THE NAKED MARRIAGE

UNDRESSING THE TRUTH ABOUT SEX, INTIMACY AND LIFELONG LOVE

DAVE WILLIS
ASHLEY WILLIS

XO
PUBLISHING

Dave and Ashley's ministry has benefited me greatly. They strive to apply God's truth in an uncompromising and yet grace-based manner. If I see they're behind it, I know it's worth my time hearing what they have to say. I know I'll be challenged, inspired and motivated to keep Jesus at the center of my marriage.

−GARY THOMAS, *Bestselling Author of Sacred Marriage and Cherish*

If you want a better sex life and a stronger marriage, then read this book! It will make an instant impact.

−BRENT EVANS, *President of MarriageToday and Founder of XO Marriage*

Dave and Ashley Willis have become some of the nation's most trusted voices on issues related to marriage. They're the real deal. Their insights are Biblically-based and incredibly practical. Their ministry can make a huge impact in your marriage and your family.

−CHRIS BROWN, *Dave Ramsey Team Speaker, Financial Coach, Pastor and Podcaster*

Dave and Ashley Wills do a great job of taking you on a journey with them. They are funny, honest and always stay true to what God's word says. Married couples that attend their conferences or read their material and apply it will take their relationship to the next level.

−LENZY CORNATZER, *Family Pastor at Crossroads Christian Church*

Dave and Ashley are some of the best marriage communicators out there. They are funny, relatable, and skilled in sharing biblical truth in a way that will help your marriage for years to come.
–*RYAN AND SELENA FREDERICK, Founders of FierceMarriage.com*

The Naked Marriage is a book every couple should read, but only if they want a BETTER sex life! Dave and Ashley take on the topic of sexual intimacy in a fresh way I haven't seen before. Every chapter is filled with practical insights for the Christian married couple who wants more for their sexual relationship.
–*MICHAEL SMALLEY, Ph.D., CEO of The Smalley Institute*

Dave and Ashley Willis communicate in The Naked Marriage the powerful insights behind what the scripture say illuminate the path to marital intimacy. This book is truly a treasure!
–*RASHAWN COPELAND, Pastor and Author*

In our marriage and sex confused culture, we're missing the voice of leaders who speak with biblical and practical truth. In The Naked Marriage, Dave and Ashley Willis provide exactly what couples need to help them grow in their marriage and in sexual and emotional intimacy. They don't shy away from the hard topics and will help many couples with the format of this new book.
–*SCOTT KEDERSHA, Director of Marriage Ministry, Watermark Community Church*

Sex is natural. Sex is fun. Sex is best when its one on one. George Michael said that and in this new book Dave and Ashley say a lot more then just that. No clue why this topic is off limits in most churches and most churches. Dive into this book to experience you best sex life now.

−CRAIG GROSS, *Founder of XXXchurch.com and Best-SexLifeNow.com*

Dave and Ashley Willis are so honest and transparent in their writings. I absorb so much from their work and will apply their teachings to my marriage, always.

−BRANDI RHODES, *Professional Wrestler, Actress and Lifestyle Blogger*

I've called Dave and Ashley Willis the 'Marriage Whisperers' and for good reason—their practical, helpful tips make successful marriage less mysterious and more accessible to all, no matter where your marriage is on the happy scale.

−NANCY FRENCH, *New York Times Bestselling Author*

Even though Catherine and I didn't come to our relationship in a very traditional way, I want to make sure I spend a lifetime with the woman I love. I know that marriage won't always be easy—that's where Dave and Ashley Willis come in. With practical and Biblical advice, they shed light on the ways that marriage can work well…and ways we can accidentally mess it up. It's a complicated world out there, and they provide a plan to navigate it well…and for a lifetime!

−SEAN LOWE, *Star of ABC's The Bachelor, Dancing with the Stars, and Bestselling Author*

One of the biggest needs in today's culture is to recapture the true depth, definition, and density of love. We've turned it into a fuzzy, emotional, Disney-esque thing, when in fact it's so much deeper and richer than that. What I love most about Dave and Ashley is they're relentless in pointing us back to that definition of love. One that fills us up, and lasts. I'm thankful for them and their words!

-JEFFERSON BETHKE, *New York Times Bestselling Author of Jesus>Religion*

Dave and Ashley's book will give you a new perspective and guide you on how to build God-centered relationships. It is easy to read and very practical. Each chapter presents a real life story that is relatable and life-changing. If you are looking to enhance your relationships and/or mend a broken heart, this is the book for you.

–PARDON NDHLOVU, *2016 Olympic Marathoner for Team Zimbabwe*

P.O. Box 59888
Dallas, Texas 75229
1-800-380-6330
or visit our website at www.marriagetoday.com

XO Publishing

Printed in the United States of America

DEDICATION

"This book is dedicated to every couple who has the faith to believe the best days of their marriage are still ahead of them."
Dave and Ashley Willis

CONTENTS

INTRODUCTION

We share a passion for helping people improve their marriages. We have worked together to create many marriage-building resources because we strongly believe that when your marriage is strong, every other aspect of your life will improve as a result. We don't claim to be experts, but we are honored to be encouragers for so many couples around the world.

We have four sons ranging in age from pre-school through middle school. Our home is filled with a lot of laughter, noise, sweat, superhero costumes, and video games. We love the Lord, we love our family and we love our jobs, because our jobs are all about helping other married couples build stronger marriages.

We're part of the team at *Marriage Today* and maybe you've seen us at an XO Marriage Conference or maybe you've seen one of our blogs or videos online. Maybe you have no idea who we are, and you just picked up this book because someone recommended or you liked the fact that it has "naked" in the title! That's cool too. Either way, we look forward to sharing some of our own journey with you.

It's hard to believe, but it's been almost twenty years since we said, "I do!"

Our love story has been a unique journey. All love stories are unique journeys because God's plan for each couple is masterfully unique. He breaks the mold with each of us, and each marriage is a lifelong path of unexpected challenges and unexpected joys. Our relationship has experienced many highs and lows along the ways, and one of the most profound joys we experience together is the joy that comes from encouraging other married couples. That's right, you are a big part of our story, and we're honored to be a small part of yours.

This book is about uncovering God's plan for you. It's about discovering the beauty of a naked marriage, which happens when a husband and wife live with complete vulnerability, transparency and trust. That's the way God intended marriage, when He made the first couple "naked and unashamed" in the Garden of Eden.

Don't settle for anything less than the life-giving, joy-filled, heart-pounding, all-in marriage God wants for you and your spouse. No matter where you've been or what you've done, you can still have it. Bring your brokenness and your fears and let's take this journey together. There are no perfect people allowed. Jesus is the only perfect part of your marriage and as we continue this journey together, we'll discover how to make His presence more profound in your relationship. You'll also learn the beautiful truth that a "perfect marriage" is just two imperfect people who refuse to give up on each other.

Marriage is a journey. The broken parts don't get fixed all at once, but all at once you can make a decision to chart a new course and start heading in a new direction. By reading this book, that's exactly what you're doing. You're resolving to set out in the best possible direction for the long-term health of your marriage and the generational legacy of your family. One page at a time and one day at a time, you're moving closer and closer to that perfect plan God has for you. Let's get started!

1

NAKED IS GOOD

Dave

I remember it like it was yesterday. I had just returned home for summer break and I was starting work at a camp before heading back to college for my senior year. Ashley and I had been talking about marriage since our third date, and the time had come to get the ring and plan a perfect evening to propose. I wanted to close the deal fast before she realized that she was way out of my league and could probably find a much better guy if she looked around.

With the help of her parents, I planned an elaborate story to give me an excuse to go and do some prep work. I told her that I needed to go visit my brother who had just broken his collarbone. I hadn't thought through my backstory well because she said she wanted to come with me, so in a panic, I blurted out, "You can't...he's naked!"

"What? Why is he naked?"—she was shocked.

"I don't know. When he's injured, he likes to be naked! I know, it's weird, but you can't come. He wouldn't want you to see him like that," I awkwardly blurted.

Ashley was disappointed and confused when I left. I had knots in my stomach from nervousness and from the guilt of just having told her a ridiculous lie. To this day, I'm terrible at lying to her, which has worked out great for our marriage.

Finally, I made it back to take her to dinner and everything was ready. She looked stunning in a red dress that brought out the beautiful tones of her strawberry-blonde hair. I kept thinking, *No way is she going to say yes. She is way out of my league!*

We went out to the nicest restaurant in town, and I paid a small fortune for a meal that I was too nervous to eat. We finally made it to the spot where I was going to pop the question. It was a place called Ashland, and the weather and scenery were beautiful. My hands were shaking as I pulled out a handwritten letter and began reading it to her. I professed my undying love and commitment to her, and I promised to always love and cherish her and to build our future on a foundation of faith in God. I got down on one knee and asked her to spend her life with me. She took a deep breath and exclaimed, "No way!" My heart sank, until I realized that it was a good "no way", and she hugged me and said, "Yes!" It was one of the happiest moments of my life and it began a journey that led us to our wedding.

We had planned a beautiful day, gone through premarital counseling, and prayed that God would bless our marriage. We were completely prepared, right? Well, in some ways, yes. In other ways—absolutely not. There are many things that I wish someone would have told us before our wedding day. You know...the real stuff. The stuff they don't talk about in premarital class at church—the *inside* scoop.

Now that we have been married for nearly twenty years, what would we say to that bright-eyed, wonder-filled, young couple in love? (Our younger selves thought we knew everything about marriage.) I think I would tell them that marriage is more complex than they realize. We wanted to be the perfect couple, but our illusions about perfection were unrealistic. We soon discovered that God's definition of a healthy marriage is often different from what we see in the world around us, because a healthy marriage is a *naked marriage*.

One of the first love lessons Ashley and I learned in our marriage was the power of a naked marriage. You probably think I'm just talking about sex right now, but there's a lot more to it than that. The sexual aspect of your marriage should be a huge priority, but true intimacy requires more than just what happens in the bedroom.

Ashley

Dave and I are passionate about what we call the *naked marriage*, but we didn't come up with this idea. God did. Not only is God passionate about marriage, but the Bible has a lot to say about marriage too. In fact, the Bible begins with a marriage— *Adam and Eve.*

In Genesis, God paints a picture of this perfect place called Eden. Here, God created Adam and Eve in His own image and they were together—it was *paradise.* "Now the man and his wife were both naked, but they felt no shame" (Genesis 2:25, NLT). This was before sin and all the baggage entered the scene. And just for a beautiful moment, we got this picture of what marriage could be—intimate, open, honest, vulnerable, and loving.

God created a couple who temporarily lived in an ideal setting with no debt, no crazy in-laws, no baggage, no stress, no fighting, and finally—no clothing! Dave likes to say, "They didn't have anything up their sleeves, because they weren't wearing any sleeves!" This first married couple was intimately connected, and they had each other's back. They were strengthened by each other's love, and their relationship was built on a solid foundation of commitment—commitment to each other and to God.

The secret-free marriage, or the *naked marriage*, is a beautiful picture of what God wants our relationship with Him to look like. Unfortunately, we live in a world where we receive conflicting pictures of what marriage is supposed to be. From the time we are little, we are bombarded with ideas and opinions of marriage.

Whether it's about sex or emotional intimacy and connec- tion, many of us struggle with feeling vulnerable, but that is what God intended—for marriage to be naked. The fear of intimacy is normal. We all carry this fear: *Am I lovable, am I worthy, would they still want me if they saw the whole me?*

Every couple wonders if they can be completely naked spiritually, emotionally, and physically. Many times, it's hard to verbalize what we like and don't like about how marriage looks, so couples are left feeling confused. When this happens, the picture of marriage starts to feel more complicated. Society continues this notion of entering marriage clueless because we are told, "It's really not about the marriage, it's about the wedding." And so, couples put all their time and resources into preparing for the wedding, but they don't give time to planning for a successful marriage. We need to enter marriage asking, "What is it really supposed to look like?"

Perhaps you look to your own parents and your own family. You may like some of the things your parents did, but maybe you have some things you want to do differently. Your spouse may also have their own ideas because of the influence of their parents.

Dave and I came from very different backgrounds. Because of what we experienced growing up, going into our marriage we had different ideas of sex and intimacy. Dave grew up in a home where his parents were always flirting with each other and being silly, and his mom was always sitting on her husband's lap, and they would hold hands. They were affectionate with one another.

While I grew up in a loving home where my parents cared about each other deeply, they were not openly affectionate with one another and they never talked to us about sex. If sex was ever mentioned it was in the context of, "Dear God! Never do it!" Actually, my wedding day was the first time my mom was willing to bring up the topic of sex. I was twenty years old when Dave and I got married and right before our ceremony, my mom looked over at me and said for the *first* time, "Well, I guess we better talk about sex." I told her it was a little late for that, because by this point what I knew about sex was through friends and health class.

Going into our marriage, Dave and I waited to have sex, but I built up my expectations of what sex was supposed to be (or not be), and I was anxious and scared. Even after having a great wedding night, I still had a lot of apprehensions about sex, and I didn't feel like I knew what I was doing. Then my anxieties were amplified when I discovered, early in our marriage, that Dave had been looking at porn. And while he quickly repented and began to rebuild trust, I still felt fearful and awkward about sex. Originally, I thought this part of our relationship would be easy and just work itself out, so I was surprised when at first it didn't. To make matters worse, I didn't always share with Dave how I was feeling, but when I discovered Dave's porn struggle, we started talking about what was going on in our lives and about our expectations.

We did have fear of intimacy and vulnerability early in our marriage, but as Dave and I travel and talk to couples, we've discovered that we aren't alone. Even if trust has been broken in your marriage, you can rebuild it. Even if you have the same hang-ups and insecurities that Dave and I had, being vulnerable (as hard as that is) is only going to help your marriage to grow closer.

Dave

Do you remember the first time you told your spouse, "I love you!"—I do. That special day is vivid in my mind...for more reasons than one.

To accurately paint the picture of this scene, you need to know it was one of the least romantic places imaginable: my dingy, dirty college dorm room. To my knowledge, my roommate hadn't washed his sheets even once in the two years I'd been living with him. We constantly sprayed Febreze and Lysol, but our best efforts to mask the stench of dirty clothes, wet towels, and old food did little to create much ambience.

My sweet mom nearly cried the first time she visited. As unpleasant as the surroundings may have been, all those unsavory details seemed to disappear when I looked at Ashley. I had never felt that way about anyone, and I figured it had to be love. I had to tell her. It felt like a volcano of unexpressed emotion was welling up in my heart and trying to come out of my mouth. I knew that if I didn't say something right then, there was a decent chance I'd end up puking on her instead. This was a defining moment and the first time I was truly vulnerable.

The look on my face must have been a combination of nausea, fear, anticipation, confusion, and joy. Ashley gave me a concerned look with those gorgeous eyes of hers and said, "What are you thinking about?"

I felt completely vulnerable and exposed, like I was standing in my underwear in front of everyone I knew. And just to be clear, I've never looked very attractive in my underwear. (The more of my body I can cover up, the more attractive it seems.) My mouth was dry, and I was having trouble forming coherent words, but I swallowed hard and gathered my strength. And with the squeaky voice of a prepubescent adolescent, I finally said, "I was thinking...I was thinking that I love you."

I got it out. It was not one of my smoothest moments, and I doubt the scene will ever be replayed in a great love story, but I got it out. I said it. She smiled at me, and without hesitation she said, "I love you too." Even though we were still in my nasty dorm room, in that moment we might as well have been on top of the Eiffel Tower with fireworks going off in the background. I had expressed my love, and that love had been reciprocated. It's amazing how free and how strong you can feel when you are completely vulnerable, and you receive *love* in exchange.

Through our years together and the different seasons of our marriage and family, our love and vulnerability has grown deeper and richer. We've gained a fuller understanding of what vulnerability really means. But vulnerability is not something that is defined by words alone. It is our choice each day to live without secrets. To live completely honest and open with our spouse—naked in every way. Everything changes for the better in our marriages when we are committed to being vulnerable with each other and *secret free*.

Ashley

A secret-free relationship creates a solid foundation of commitment—commitment to each other and to God. During premarital counseling, our pastor opened his Bible and read,

> *"A person standing alone can be attacked and defeated, but two can stand back-to-back and conquer. Three are even better, for a triple-braided cord is not easily broken"*
> Ecclesiastes 4:12 (NLT)

Up until that moment, I honestly never thought much about this verse, but after one of our sessions, our pastor gave us a rather unusual wedding gift. He handed us a real triple-braided cord.

He then explained the verse and said that this illustrated a strong marriage in which the husband, wife, and God each represent a strand of the cord, with God being the heartiest strand. This kind of cord is hard to break and extremely secure, but the cord is only as strong as each strand. If one strand is weakened or cut off, the cord loses some of its strength and with enough weight it will eventually fray and break down completely.

The longer we are married and work with married couples, the more we see the truth of this verse played out. I am not sure where you might be in your faith, but I encourage you to keep God at the center of your marriage. How do we keep God as the primary *strand* in our marriage? We do this by making our personal relationship with Christ a priority. We strive to know Him more by going to church and reading our Bibles, and we make prayer a consistent part of our daily lives. When we keep our relationship with God as our top priority, our minds and hearts are more prepared to approach our spouse with the love and devotion he or she deserves, and we essentially keep our strands connected to the master strand. When this happens, our *cord*s of marriage remain strong.

When God painted this picture of a *naked marriage*, He was revealing to us something more than just sexual intimacy; He was revealing the importance of having complete transparency, vulnerability, acceptance, and intimacy at every level of the relationship. I'm certainly not advocating that we all walk around naked all day (although Dave and I do think most marriages would benefit from more naked time), but I am suggesting that we all need to become more intentional about reconnecting with that true intimacy that Adam and Eve got a taste of in the Garden of Eden. Marital love has to be completely open, honest, and transparent. Secrets are as dangerous as lies and can rob your relationship of intimacy and trust. Love, by its very nature, *is* honest, and this is especially important to the sacred bond of trust in marriage.

Through our years together and the different seasons of our marriage and family, our love has grown deeper and richer. We've also gained a fuller understanding of what marriage really means. It's not something that can be defined by feelings or captured by words alone. God created marriage to be a transformative force in every aspect of our lives, and once we understand and embrace it, our marriage will come into clearer focus and will grow in deeper levels of intimacy and vulnerability.

Dave

Ashley and I interact with thousands of couples and we see a trend of marriages ending because of *incompatibility*. There's a huge modern myth that divorce due to *incompatibility* will solve all the problems you're facing in your marriage, but the reality is, divorce usually creates more problems than it solves. Instead of committing to the covenant of marriage, more and more couples choose to end it. It's not that there's anything wrong with marriage. In fact, marriage is more important than ever. The problem is our modern culture has taken this beautiful gift of marriage and gone about it in the wrong way. We're missing the point of marriage, and families are being built without a solid foundation.

Why are fewer people choosing to marry when studies consistently show that marriages reduce crime, give increased stability to children, increase life expectancy, increase emotional happiness, and produce more wealth? The temptation and anxiety associated with marriage is so strong these days that people are afraid to make the commitment and more and more people simply choose to stay single. But God created marriage to be much more than cohabitating; it's a covenant. We need to build marriage upon our commitments. The strongest couples have learned that marriage means choosing to love each other even on those days when you struggle to like each other. When both spouses commit to be vulnerable and secret free, the marriage thrives.

Ashley

Often, we tend to think that all marriage problems stem from a big breach of trust. However, many times the lack of love isn't because of a one-time sin but an ongoing pattern of behavior leading to what Dave and I call a "cable-company marriage." I know that probably sounds pretty random, so let me explain.

Have you ever noticed how cable companies treat their customers with amazing care and attentiveness when they're first trying to seal the deal? However, once they've got you, the introductory rates are replaced with much more expensive rates and the customer service takes a nosedive, which makes you want to trade in your old cable company for a new one. The cable TV industry seems focused on a model of treating people really well at first but then taking them for granted in the long run.

Sadly, a lot of marriages operate this way too. In the beginning, when the couple is trying to win each other's hearts, they roll out the red carpet. They give the very best of themselves, but it doesn't last long. Once the day-to-day reality of life together sets in, they stop doing all those things they did in the beginning. They take each other for granted, and it isn't long before they both start longing for something new where they'll be treated well again.

It doesn't have to be this way! Marriages should grow stronger with time. Couples should continue pursuing, encouraging, and loving each other through all the seasons of the relationship.

If you find yourself in a cable-company marriage right now, don't lose hope. Don't throw away your relationship just to start a new one with someone else and repeat the same cycle. Make a commitment to transform your marriage. Stop taking each other for granted. Your best days together can still be ahead of you and not behind you.

Dave and I have discovered that being married is more complex than we naively assumed it would be in the beginning. We both had a desire to become a perfect spouse, but we soon discovered that God's definition of a healthy marriage is often different from what we see in the world around us. We all have in our minds what a perfect marriage looks like, but a marriage where there is commitment and vulnerability is the *best* kind.

The beauty of a *naked marriage* happens when a husband and wife live with complete vulnerability, transparency, and trust. That's the way God intended marriage when He made the first couple "naked and unashamed." And though you probably shouldn't be naked in public, unless you'd like to get an arrest and some awkward posts about you on social media, God still wants us to have naked marriages today. It is our hope and prayer that as you and your spouse read these pages, you both will discover how to make His presence more profound in your relationship, and that you'll learn the beautiful truth that a perfect marriage—a naked marriage—is just two imperfect people who refuse to give up on each other.

Dave

In the *naked marriage*, everything changes for the better. But before that can happen, there must be commitment to vulnerability and to *nakedness* in every way. Without real vulnerability and honesty, there can be no real love.

One year, our kids had an ongoing project of building a fort in the empty lot next to our house. Almost every day after school, they would meet up with the other neighborhood kids and look for scrap materials to add to their beloved masterpiece. It was really nothing more than some old crates and cardboard stacked together. Every time a storm came, the whole thing fell apart, and they would start the whole process over again.

I've never been much help on the fort project because I'm terrible with tools. Ashley's dad is a guy who can build and fix anything, so when Ashley married me, she assumed all men had the same skill set. I wish I had those skills, but when I try swinging a hammer, stuff gets broken. Ashley is both the beautiful one and the handy one in our relationship.

The boys wish I was better at construction so I could help them build forts. I do my best to help them gather materials, but my most valuable contribution thus far has been a single bit of engineering advice. I told them the fort was going to keep collapsing until they built it securely on a solid foundation.

Many marriages resemble that old fort. Maybe there's a lot of effort going into building the marriage, but it still seems to struggle—seemingly falling apart. Some marriages fall apart due to a lack of effort, but many more marriages fail for the same reasons the boys' fort kept collapsing. The husband and wife built their relationship with the wrong tools and with no solid foundation.

Matthew 7:24–27 contains one of Jesus' most famous teachings. He tells the story of a wise builder and a foolish builder. This wise builder took the time to build his house on a foundation of solid rock, while the foolish builder took the fast and easy route and built his house on sand.

From the outside, both houses looked the same, but the difference was revealed when a storm came. The strong winds and rains beat against both houses, and the house without a solid foundation collapsed. The house built on the rock stood strong.

When you read magazines and look at the examples of marriages in pop culture, it seems as though many people are content to build a marriage with no solid foundation. These shaky marriages are usually based on fickle feelings, codependent insecurities, mutual convenience or lust. When the storms of life come, the marriage can't survive.

Feelings are real, but we should never let them rule us. When we build our marriage on our feelings instead of our commitment, the marriage will be shaky at best because there was no solid foundation. There's nothing wrong with feelings. They're an important part of life, but they were never intended to be our compass or our *foundation*. Feelings are fickle.

The strongest marriages, however, are built on a foundation of love, vulnerability, and commitment. The strength of your commitment will always determine the strength of your marriage. God's definition of marriage is rooted in the concept of commitment and vulnerability. When you said, "I do," to your spouse, you weren't just expressing your current feelings; you were making a promise of commitment that will ultimately be your legacy of love.

Marriage, by its very nature, is a conscious choice to selflessly put the needs of your spouse ahead of your own preferences or comforts. No marriage can survive unless it is rooted in rock-solid commitment and honest vulnerability.

As a pastor for many years, I had the privilege of officiating wedding ceremonies. It's such an honor to stand in that sacred moment with a bride and groom as they exchange vows and rings and enter into the holy covenant of marriage. One of the Bible passages I often read at wedding ceremonies comes from Ruth 1:16–17:

> *But Ruth replied, "Don't ask me to leave you and turn back. Wherever you go, I will go; wherever you live, I will live. Your people will be my people, and your God will be my God. Wherever you die, I will die, and there I will be buried. May the Lord punish me severely if I allow anything but death to separate us!"*
> *(NLT)*

These words beautifully capture the commitment necessary for a strong marriage. God wants to create a generational impact through your marriage. The level at which your marriage will make an eternal impact is defined by your level of commitment to pursuing and possessing a *naked marriage*. There is no relationship more sacred than your marriage, so treasure your spouse. Never let anyone or anything take the place of priority your spouse should hold in your heart. Marriage is one of God's greatest gifts.

2

NAKED COMMUNICATION

Ashley

When Dave and I married, I thought that Dave would gradually become an expert mind reader of sorts when it came to me. I assumed this was just something that happened when you got married. I thought that if I rolled my eyes enough or stomped around enough Dave would automatically know what I was thinking or what I needed. I didn't have to tell him what I felt because *of course* he could read my mind. He is supposed to know me—he *should* know me. But Dave had this idea that whatever I said was what I meant, so if I said I was okay then he could just go back to watching SportsCenter because I said I was *okay*! Well this kind of thinking (and utter lack of communication) wasn't working.

There was one word that got Dave and me into a lot of trouble and that was a particular four-letter "f-word." Well, it might not be the f-word that you are thinking of but for us the f-word was—*fine*. For example, I would tell Dave I was fine, but I was anything but fine, and I might as well have been cussing at him. For us, it was a dangerous word and it ended conversations instead of starting them. For Dave, *fine* was guy code for, "I had a long day. I'm out of words and I don't want to talk." Or I would say *fine,* but I was trying to mask how I really felt.

We realized that when we said *fine,* we were really saying, "I'm **F**aking, I'm **I**gnoring, I'm **N**eglecting, and I'm **E**vading." You may have words like this in your marriage too that you need to remove from your vocabulary. There was one key moment in our relationship when we realized how dangerous this word was for us.

We had two little ones at the time, and we had just moved to a new city. It had been a hard move. For any of you who have moved before, you know how hard it can be adjusting to a new town and to new jobs, especially when you have young children. I call times like this "sandpaper seasons." It's like everything (and everyone) is rubbing you the wrong way. So, one morning, I was climbing the ladder to hang a curtain rod and I was having a hard time. I couldn't get the drill to work right and the screw was going in at a funny angle, and I was just feeling frustrated. Normally, I like home improvements, decorating, and getting settled in a new home, but this morning it just wasn't working.

As I was stomping up and down the ladder, in walks Dave. He was smiling and looking fresh for the morning. He looked at me. "Hey sweetie. I was thinking about going for a run. It's such a beautiful day." I looked up at him and grumped, "Fine!" like I was cussing at him. He, however, took me at my word that I was truly *fine* and so off he went on his run. The whole time he was gone I was fuming. I was having an argument with Dave in my mind the entire time—and I was winning it!

Finally, Dave came home all refreshed from his run and he looked down at the curtain rod that I had left on the floor and said, "Oh wow! The curtain rod is still not up?" At that moment my head spun around like I was from *The Exorcist* and I released word-vomit all over Dave. I had smoke coming out my ears as I yelled, "I can't even look at you right now!" Suddenly, Dave realized that I really wasn't *fine* after all. As I watched Dave's expression turn from confusion into shock, I realized how ridiculous it was for me to expect him to read my mind and I thought, *Oh my goodness, my husband was listening to my words and believed me when I said I was fine!* He really thought I was fine, and I could have just told him that I wasn't, and I needed his help! We stopped saying the f-word that day.

For some reason, many of us stop effectively using our words when we marry. We make assumptions that our spouse gets us, so we don't need to honestly communicate with them anymore. We think they know all our thoughts, and so we don't need to say anything. Or we assume that we know what they are thinking or feeling and so we don't really need to listen to what they are saying. When this starts happening, communication breaks down and the vulnerability and intimacy in our marriage begins to crumble and we are left with these two people coexisting—not really engaging in a real marriage—more like business partners or roommates. But God doesn't want this for us. He wants us to have a beautiful partnership with one another. Therefore, we need to stop making assumptions.

I remember how important it was for me to learn not to make assumptions about Dave, but I also remember a time when it was vital for me to be completely vulnerable in my communication with him.

One night, I could barely breathe. Quietly, I padded my way to the bathroom. Pulling my hair back, I hung my head over the toilet and waited—just like so many nights before. But this time nothing came. My chest still tight, I crept my way back to our bed and slid beside Dave.

Holding my breath, my heart pounding in my ears, I waited. Waited to see if I had woken him. Waited to see if I would have to share with him my secret. Waited to see if he would finally know that I wasn't enough—at least that is how I felt. He didn't wake up. I was spared at least one more night from having to confess to him. I thought, *I don't need to tell him what's going on with me because I can handle this myself, and maybe tomorrow will be different? Maybe I will feel better?*

Nights bled into days and days turned into months. Do you remember the character from *Charlie Brown* with the little cloud over his head that followed him everywhere he went? Well, that was me, only my little dust cloud was suffocating. I couldn't sleep, I couldn't laugh, I couldn't breathe, and I felt like I couldn't live. No matter how hard I tried, no matter how much I forced myself to think "happy thoughts," nothing was working. Terrified of this woman looking back at me in the mirror, I tried to hide my depression and anxiety from Dave. I thought, *If he finds out how much I'm struggling then there is no way he will want to stay married to me.*

One night, I was at my lowest point. I had just finished throwing up and I was still shaking, but I decided tonight I would finally tell Dave what was happening. I was so nervous as I woke him up. "Dave, Dave…I need you to wake up and pray for me." He rubbed the sleep out of his eyes and sat up in bed. Through my tears, I told him that I was paralyzed by fear and anxiety, unable to sleep and overwhelmed with depression. I shared how scared I was that he would reject me if he really knew how I was doing. Without hesitating, Dave took me in his arms and he began to pray for me. As I listened to his prayer, I cried with relief. He hadn't rejected me. He wasn't angry or disappointed with me. I was so scared to communicate to him my true feelings, but because I did, he was now able to love and support me in a way that I desperately needed. And while my depression and anxiety didn't instantly disappear, I learned a lesson that night that I will never forget—the power of *naked* communication. This experience changed the way we communicated and when a couple changes the way they communicate, and they get real and honest with each other, then the relationship goes to the next level.

To this day, I am thankful I had the courage to honestly communicate to Dave my struggle with depression and anxiety. He was able to love me through it and to pray for me. Today, I am free, but I don't think I would be had I not been *naked* enough to tell Dave everything I was going through. In the naked marriage, we communicate openly and honestly about everything that is going on in our lives.

Dave

"We will speak the truth in love, growing in every way more and more like Christ"
Ephesians 4:15 (NLT)

One of the core values in the Willis household is honest communication. And our kids know that they can get in trouble for lots of things but lying tops the list of deadly sins. We put value on honesty because we want our kids to realize that love is built on trust and open communication. Ashley and I believe that if we want to keep our family and marriage strong, we've always got to tell one another the truth.

But Ashley and I went through several years when the kids learned this *tell-the-truth* lesson so well that it nearly backfired on us. They assumed that because the truth was so important, if they considered something to be true, they could say it aloud. On the surface, this doesn't seem like a bad thing until we had some embarrassing interactions in public. For example, here are some *truths* that my children spoke to strangers in public:

"Wow, you have a huge belly!"

"You look really old like Yoda."

"You smell funny."

"Why are you dressed like that? Are you poor?"

"Are you going to feed milk to the baby from your nipples?" (That last one actually referred to me. Apparently, I have *man boobs*.)

As you can imagine, we preferred to keep these kinds of phrases from being blurted out in public to complete strangers. My first thought was, *Let's just stop taking the kids to Walmart!* For some reason, a lot of these incidents seemed to happen at Walmart. The kids seem to behave better when we're at Target.

We knew that isolating the kids in solitary confinement until adulthood wouldn't work, so we needed a new strategy that kept the emphasis on truth but also put a filter in the process. Our friends had a policy that their kids weren't allowed to say anything to anyone unless it met three criteria: it had to be true, kind, and necessary—TKN. We thought this was a great idea, so we taught this policy to our boys. We told our kids that communicating truth was vital, but the truth alone wasn't enough. You could say something that was technically right, but if you said it without love and compassion, you were still wrong.

We quickly got some real-world testing grounds to try the new policy. We were at the grocery store, and the boys were hovering around the cart looking for candy to sneak in while I wasn't looking. An elderly lady limped past on her cane, and I held my breath as the boys started to say something. They quickly caught themselves and bit their tongues. Then, while she was still just a few steps away, they shouted with pride, "Dad! We did it! That really old lady just walked by, and we didn't even tell her that she looked old like Yoda!" I patted the boys on the head while giving an awkward smile to the sweet lady who heard every word of their commentary. Like most life lessons, this was a work in progress.

Speaking the truth in love to our spouse doesn't mean you should never communicate a painful truth. In fact, the Bible teaches that painful truths from a friend can be trusted. This principle holds true if your spouse has developed dangerous or self-destructive habits. In naked communication, couples have the courage to speak the truth in love. The truth isn't always comfortable, but it is always necessary. Naked communication is vital for marriage. God created marriage to be a relationship of complete unity and transparency. Deception of any kind will undermine the foundation of the marriage covenant. Your marriage will never be stronger than your trust in each other and this happens through *naked* communication.

If you struggle with communication, you are not alone! Maybe, you are like Ashley and I were early in our marriage thinking communication would flow naturally, but the reality is that it doesn't. We need to talk—with words—to one another. Put down the phone. Turn off the television. Close the laptop. We must remove distractions when it comes to effective communication with our spouse. Give them your *eyes*.

I struggle with this too. God made us to crave connection and nothing replaces face-to-face conversation. Let's give our spouse our best attention, not a half-hearted glance from a device. Friends, let's put it all away and share our heart with our spouse. Dream together. Laugh together. Cry together. Share your fears together. Daily heart-to-heart conversation is the cornerstone of true intimacy.

Ashley

Dave and I both have college degrees in communication, so we thought this part of our relationship would be a breeze, but we quickly learned early on that communication is something you must work at. It doesn't come naturally for anybody. Every husband and every wife must intentionally listen and clearly communicate. Some of the ways Dave and I promote conversation in our marriage is by spending time going on walks, going on drives, going out to dinner, and being in settings that allow us talk time.

The settings for *talk time* can be anywhere. As the parents of four young boys, one of our favorite places for conversation is the YMCA. It offers two hours of free childcare, which is worth its weight in gold. While our kids are playing and having fun, we spend the first thirty minutes sitting down and having a cup of coffee and talking with each other. We make sure the kids know what we're doing, to plant that seed in their young minds, that Mommy and Daddy love each other and make their marriage a priority.

A lot of folks walk in ready for their workout and see us lounging on a loveseat and they sometimes give us funny looks like we're wasting our time. But for us, it's one of the most productive moments of the day. Sure, we would probably have smaller love handles if we spent that extra half hour on the treadmill, but I wouldn't trade that time in conversation with Dave for the world. Making time for each other a consistent priority has been one of the most significant decisions we've made for our marriage.

Recently, a guy who works at the YMCA made a point to stop and tell us that his daughter and son-in-law were having marriage problems. He told them about our little "gym date" routine and bought them a gym membership. He encouraged them to take advantage of the childcare not only to work out but to have time to communicate and work out their relationship. That was a huge compliment to Dave and me and a challenge to continue developing the types of marriage-building habits that are worth imitation.

Getting a marriage in shape isn't all that different from getting your body in shape, but it must start with honest communication. You don't get out of shape all at once and you won't get back into shape all at once, but you can make a decision to alter your course and start moving in a healthier direction by developing healthy habits. Over time, those consistent investments of time and conversation will bring health to your marriage. Your love handles may not get any smaller, but your love and understanding for each other will grow and that is what counts the most.

Dave

Marriage, by God's design, is the foundation of the family. Building stronger marriages will lead to stronger families, which leads to stronger communities, and ultimately, a better world. Marriage is sacredly designed to display God's kingdom on earth. When marriages improve, nearly everything else improves as a result. But when marriages are hurting, society suffers.

Ashley and I recently sat down with a young couple from our church. The military moved them to our area, so they didn't have a local family support system. Within the first minutes of our meeting, the wife was crying. The stress of the move had taken its toll on this young family. The husband's long hours and pressing new responsibilities increased the tension at home. They both needed the marriage to be a source of strength and encouragement during this difficult time, but the foundation of their relationship was crumbling.

The husband and wife were dealing with the stress in their own ways. They weren't communicating with each other. They were drifting further apart instead of facing their struggles side by side. They desperately wanted to make the marriage work, but they weren't sure where or how to begin supporting each other. It was hard for them to have vulnerability in their communication.

We prayed with them and reminded them that with Christ as their foundation, they could weather any storm. We told them that they didn't need to face their challenges alone because God calls us to carry each other's burdens and to find healing and support within a biblical community. We gave them some resources to help them begin to communicate with each other. Also, we recommended a good Christian counselor who could help them have open talk time, while giving ongoing support and guidance. Over time, they experienced healing and transformation in their marriage. Now, they can share honestly what is going on in their hearts through daily communication, and this has helped to heal their marriage.

Each week countless couples just like this one appear to have everything together, but often there's a hidden reality. Many marriages are hurting because of a breakdown in communication. Broken relationships can be healed, and strong marriages can grow even stronger through honest communication in the *naked marriage*. We've learned that all married couples need encouragement and practical tools to help them with communication, but most married couples don't know where to begin.

Naked communication isn't easy. In fact, it requires emotional and mental nakedness. We're born naked and crying. We're fully exposed and it's cold and uncomfortable at first, and naked vulnerability in marriage can feel like this at first. It's what we long for and what we're created for, but in a world that has taught us to wear masks, it feels unnatural at first to bare our soul to someone else. The naked marriage pushes through any initial awkwardness that comes with vulnerability, and it is worth it. Make talk time together a priority. Budget for a consistent date night. Time is the currency of your relationship, so consistently invest time for communication into your marriage!

Ashley

Another way that we honor naked communication in our marriages is by considering our spouse's feelings in every decision we make. Every decision we make impacts our spouse in some way. This is vital to remember because our decisions are communicating our love and respect, or they are unintentionally communicating a lack of love and respect.

Recently, a friend asked me if we could get together for a girls' night out and I naturally replied as I always do to these invitations, "I'd love to! Let me ask Dave first and I will let you know..." My friend rolled her eyes and laughed under her breath as she replied, "Really? You need your husband's *permission*? Why? My husband and I never ask for permission. I just do my own thing. And he does his thing."

I couldn't believe she said that. Why would this even be an issue? Sure, there are times I honestly don't want to ask Dave's permission, but I do it anyway because he is my husband. I love him. We are one. Our individual lives are interdependent. Therefore, every personal decision we make automatically brings joint consequences. We don't always ask permission about minor things like what to wear or what to eat, but we have always consulted each other on most everything else, and I like it. It works for us.

Despite my own feelings about the matter, my friend's response got me thinking: *Am I the norm or is asking your spouse's permission before making a scheduling decision or major lifestyle change a rare thing?* I don't know. I do know that Dave and I have a better marriage because of it.

Asking each other's permission communicates love and respect to your spouse. Whenever Dave asks me if he can go somewhere and do something, I feel loved, cherished, and respected. We are married after all. Why wouldn't we consult each other first before placing something on the calendar, applying for a new job, or moving? These things affect both of us, so we need to discuss it first out of respect for one another.

Asking permission also ensures less conflict. The phrase, "Just do it and ask for forgiveness later," doesn't work in marriage. We need to ask each other first so it will be less likely for us to fight about a decision later. When we make a decision together beforehand, no matter what the outcome may be, we can stay unified and resist pointing fingers at one another later.

Some may argue that asking for permission creates a marriage that is like a parent-child relationship, but that isn't true when *both* ask for it. Please let me be clear—it is not healthy or acceptable for one partner to constantly have to ask the other for permission when the partner being asked goes off and does whatever he/she pleases. This is manipulative and unloving and can lead to abusive behavior. Whenever we go to our spouse to consult with him/her on a decision, we both walk away empowered. It doesn't mean that we couldn't make that particular decision on our own; it just means that we want to be united in our decisions.

We love and respect our spouse enough to communicate with them, seeking his/her guidance and desire to make a collective decision. However, there will certainly be times when the husband and wife are at a standstill in communication. In this case, the Bible tells us that the husband should make the call:

> *"For wives, this means submit to your husbands as to the*
> *Lord. For a husband is the head of his wife as Christ is the*
> *head of the church. He is the Savior of his body, the church"*
> *Ephesians 5:22–23 (NLT)*

This isn't because the husband is smarter or should be a dictator; it's because he carries a heavier (God-given) responsibility to carry the accountability for certain decisions. Support him and have his back.

When we communicate and ask our partner's permission before deciding to do things like have a girls' night out, go to the game with the guys, take on another job, change jobs, switch daycares, go back to school, or serve on the PTA, we get more perspective and insight from each other and make a more informed decision. We help each other weigh the pros and cons to decide if something is a good fit or the right time. Sure, some of the scenarios I listed are bigger decisions than others, but all are important enough to clearly communicate as a couple.

Sadly, I hear from too many married couples who are stuck in a lonely unengaged existence. Some marriages are nothing more than roommates living separate lives like passing ships in the night. They wake up, say hello, go to work without a call or text to one another all day, come home, run the kids to where they need to go, eat dinner without a word or in separate places, maybe meet up with a friend or focus all their attention on the kids at night, and then go to bed—no communication, no vulnerability. What happened? They stopped engaging in the everyday moments. They stopped talking. They stopped sharing—stopped trying. They assumed they could do marriage without communication—all on their own.

Dave

Communication in marriage is important, and my wife Ashley's voice is the sweetest sound in the world to me! I enjoy listening to her singing, whispering, flirting, or talking about nearly any subject in the world. While I always enjoy her voice, there are certain statements she communicates that make my heart race and put a big smile on my face. I know that every man is different, and every marriage is different, but I've been working with married couples long enough to recognize some clear consistencies in what every husband needs to hear.

When a wife communicates that she trusts her husband's judgment, she puts more wind in his sail than she even knows. I'm going to let you in on a little secret. We men are usually more insecure than we look. We're always wondering if we measure up and if you (our wife) think we're capable and trustworthy. When your husband knows you believe in him, he is at his best. Build him up with your words. Let him know you think he's the man and that you believe in him and trust his choices and his motives. Your trust communicates respect and he needs respect more than anything else.

Even the most confident man is secretly desperate for his wife's respect. When a husband feels respected by his wife, he believes he can take on the world. When he feels that his wife doesn't believe in him, he will carry deep, hidden wounds. The smallest act of affirmation like laughing at his cheesy "dad jokes" can make his confidence soar, while the smallest cutting remark or rejection can crush his spirit. Your respect (of lack of it) has immense power to build him up or tear him down.

Maybe your husband isn't acting very respectable right now, so you feel entitled to withhold your respect until he earns it. This is an understandable perspective, but it's also a wrong one. A lack of respect rarely motivates a man to improve, but finding something in him to praise and respect will motivate him to earn and build your belief in him.

Our good friend Shaunti Feldhahn is a bestselling author

and brilliant social researcher. Her research revealed that most men would rather hear the phrase "Thank you" than the words "I love you." It's not that men don't want to feel loved, but it's that men tend to feel most loved when they feel appreciated. Women clearly want to feel respected and appreciated as well, but women tend to prefer feeling adored and pursued, while men tend to prefer feeling respected and appreciated. Communicating that you appreciate all he does for your family strengthens your marriage.

Okay, this is *naked communication*, so we can't leave out that he would love to hear (in your sexiest voice), *"I'm wearing new panties. Do you want to see them?"* This one is a little tongue-in-cheek, but as a man, I can promise you that when you say anything sexually suggestive or seductive to your husband, it will make his day. He's thinking about sex even more than you think he is, and when you're the one who initiates, he feels desired, respected, excited, and connected to you. He wants to know you've never outgrown your crush on him. There are plenty of other statements men want to hear, but if you'll start with these, you'll be on the right track.

Your husband needs you to initiate sex and he needs you to be receptive when he initiates it. He thinks about sex all the time. No matter what he's doing at this exact moment, he would probably much rather be making love to you and he's most likely thinking about it right now. The average man has a sexual thought at least once per minute every waking hour of the day. Men who are happiest with their wives almost always cite strong sexual satisfaction as one of the major reasons.

As a quick disclaimer, some guys have a lower sex drive, and this can happen for all kinds of reasons including low testosterone, depression, exhaustion, and a myriad of other factors. If your husband's drive or desire seems low, don't take it personally. Talk about it and work together to find solutions. If your desire seems low, take the same approach. Talk about it and work together to find solutions.

Ladies, your husband wants to communicate to you that you're his best friend and he wants you to see him as your best friend too. Most women have a group of female friends who provide emotional support, conversation, and deep friendship, but most men don't have this same kind of closeness with other men. We have golfing buddies or a fantasy football league, but the typical man considers his wife to be his best friend (or at least he wants her to be). Your husband wants you to have friends and to get with your girls, but he wants to be your very best friend.

He wants to be the one you come to first to talk about good news (or bad news). He wants to be the one you're escaping to, not someone you're escaping from. He wants to share adventures with you and create enduring memories with you. The strongest marriages are between two best friends who can talk about and share everything.

Men, if you're reading this, before you start nudging your wife, I want to give you a few tips. One of the biggest ways that we husbands sabotage our friendship with our wives is through our tone and *how* we communicate to her. The tone of your words will shape the tone of your friendship and your marriage. Be tender with her. She wants to see your soft side. She'll feel safest with you when you are speaking to her most tenderly. And while you're speaking with that loving tone, be sure to remind her of your love for her. Let her know that you're captivated by her and that you have eyes only for her. Let her know how lucky you feel, how thankful you are that she chose you, and how excited you are about dreaming new dreams together with her for the rest of your lives. Value vulnerable communication and let the tone of your words reflect the love you have for her. Ask your wife if this is true for her. It will spark some great conversations and help you learn more about each other in the process.

Ashley

We wear a lot of hats as women. Many of us have husbands, kids, jobs, homes, errands to run, kids' sports to commute to, and the list goes on. We could spend a whole day taking care of each of these, but we have to prioritize. Most days, women try to do just that—take care of our loved ones and the many duties that come along with them. (Oops, I forgot to put ourselves on the list, but this is often how it goes.)

For husbands, it is important for you to understand what your wives are thinking and feeling. Often, the wife is thinking, *Would he still choose me?* But, she is terrified to ask you. This thought has nothing to do with confidence or even how we look. It has everything to do with the relationship we have with our husbands. We want to know that he still thinks we are "smokin' hot," as my husband says. We want to know that he only has eyes for us. Women long to be adored and prized, whether we are ill, pregnant, a little heavy or too thin. As wives, we are willing to do things to make ourselves attractive to our spouses and we want them to notice. Husbands, we see the way you look at us and we hear your words. We want to know that you find us desirable on all levels: sexually (tell your wife you love her body), mentally (tell your wife you love the way she thinks), and emotionally (tell your wife you love her heart). Communicate to her through your words that you love being with her.

Just like the husbands, wives want to do the best job they can at their jobs. Wives work hard, and they want their hard work to pay off. It is difficult to juggle our many duties. As a wife and mother, I have felt *mommy guilt* when it comes to balancing duties at work and home. We want to be the best wife and mother possible while also having a successful career, if we are working outside of the home. It is a daily struggle and we need to hear our husbands say that they notice and appreciate our efforts.

Marriage is a blessing and we want to get it right. Husbands, we want to know that we are meeting your needs on all levels as much as we can. Many times, we are willing to communicate our needs with our husbands more than they are willing to share their needs with us. We aren't mind readers! The more honest we can be with each other and the more we openly communicate, the better. So, husbands, let us know, so we can be the best wives possible.

Am I enough? This is what your wife is really thinking. Sometimes, I don't feel like there is enough of me to go around, and it is exhausting. When I was teaching, I would wake up and pour into my husband and kids and spend some time in prayer. Once I arrived at school, I would pour into my students. When I got back home, I would make dinner for my family, run my kids to their various activities and end the day by pouring into my husband and kids once again. I was honestly a shell of a person. I poured out all day into the ones I love, doing something I loved to do, but I was completely spent. I would often lie in bed and think, *Am I enough?* I think many women find themselves in the same boat. We often do so much but have so little to show for it at the time.

And while it has often been said that men want respect and women want to be loved, I think that women have a strong desire for respect as well. We want to know that our husbands, kids, friends, and coworkers respect us. We don't like to be disrespected just like anyone else. And sometimes, not getting a break can make us feel disrespected or taken for granted. A break for us could be a date night with our hubby, a girls' night out with our friends, or just a lazy, quiet night watching our favorite television shows while eating a big scoop of ice cream or drinking a glass of wine, or hey, let's be real—both! For some reason, wives feel guilty about needing this time, but everyone needs time to chill. Taking a couple of hours a week to reconnect with our husband, our friends, or even ourselves is needed to keep the lines of communication open.

As a Christian, I think this might be the most important

question I ask myself, *Am I making a difference?* No matter where you might be in your faith, I truly believe that God designed every one of us with a significant purpose on earth. Whether big or small, each of us has something good to offer the world. As women, we want to know that all the time and effort we put into our family, friendships, churches, charities/ministries, and work are achieving a greater purpose and making the world a better place. Start the conversation and ask your wife if this is true for her—you might be surprised. Enjoy the conversation!

Dave

And on a final note, most frustrations in marriage come either directly or indirectly from a breakdown in communication between husband and wife. Men and women both contribute to the communication breakdown in different ways. For men, the breakdown often comes through a lack of communication. Our wives need for us to talk to them, and not just the way we talk about the weather or football with our guy friends. They need us to share the details of our day. In reverse, listen carefully to what she is trying to communicate to you. Speak with truth and love and listen with respect and compassion. If you'll make communication a priority, I believe every other aspect of your marriage will begin to improve!

3

NAKED FIGHTS

Dave

Ashley is a refined, classy, lovely woman who grew up in a house full of girls. By contrast, I was basically a caveman raised in a house full of guys. Our family backgrounds were very different, which required big adjustments for us both after we married.

For instance, I never use clippers on my toenails. This is something she discovered after we were married, and it didn't seem weird to me. I always thought, *Why would you want to take something sharp and put it on your toes?* When my toenails start getting too long, I just pick at them, leaving sharp, jagged edges. I am like Wolverine from *X-Men*, except the claws grow out of my feet instead of my hands. I know what you're thinking, and you're right. It's a disgusting habit.

One night, we were sound asleep. Around 2:00 a.m. I woke up to the sound of Ashley screaming out in pain. I was terrified! I was confused; I stumbled around thinking there was an intruder in the house. It was pure chaos.

We turned the lights on, and her leg was bleeding. I thought someone had broken into our house and stabbed my beautiful wife in the leg. In our delusional state, we started trying to piece together all the evidence, and we realized there was blood on *me* as well: on my big toe. We finally deciphered the clues and solved the mystery. I was the intruder, and my disgusting toenail was the weapon!

Looking back on that crazy night brings a lot of laughter, but truthfully how we handle hardships, especially hardships we bring into the marriage because of our own unlovable flaws, determines the level of nakedness in our marriage.

Ashley

This is so true. While my leg getting cut isn't necessarily a hardship, it is a funny way to see how our flaws can unintentionally hurt our spouse and cause tension in the marriage. There have been several times in our marriage of almost twenty years that we've experienced various forms of hardship. One tough season that comes to mind happened about eight years ago when we decided to move states. We were willingly leaving a place that we loved, but very excited about starting our adventure in a new place. The moment we got there, I felt loneliness creeping in. We were staying in a tiny rental house right beside some water and that was especially hard since I had two extremely loud and active small boys who couldn't swim. Dave was busy at his new job and I was trying to hold down the fort at home with young children. As the months slowly crept by, Dave and I both felt weary and uncomfortable with our new city. It was a tough adjustment.

There were even times when I was resentful toward Dave because it seemed like he was adjusting better than I was. Still, I continued to trudge on through the long days at home with my restless boys, feeling lost and alone. The tension between us began to rise because we gradually stopped being intentional about telling each other our true feelings. I think both of us were so exhausted at the end of the day that we just couldn't even find the words. Eventually, this bad habit caught up with us. We both became so edgy toward one another and we weren't prioritizing date nights or time together like we once did. The relational dynamic between us was becoming more sinister by the day, but we wanted things to be better.

Finally, I remember Dave coming to me with tired eyes one day. He grabbed my hands and he said, "Sweetie, this has been a really hard move for both of us. I don't know why, but it just is. I hate the tension between us. What do you think would make things better for us?" I was relieved to hear him say those words. I wasn't alone in my frustration. Dave felt it too. Tears welled up in my eyes as I poured out my heart to him. I told him how much I missed my friends and family. I expressed my frustration with the boys not listening. I asked Dave how things were going at work and he talked about some frustrations he was experiencing there. Neither of us held anything back. It felt so good to just let it all out and to call this season what it really was—hard. It was good to know that we both had each other's back and that we could talk about how we were doing instead of fighting against each other.

Friends, when we are going through a tough season (and we all will at some point), we must resist the urge to face it alone, allowing resentment to take hold of our hearts. This will help you to endure hard seasons while also keeping your marriage strong. We need to go to our spouse and tell them what is on our mind and heart. Tell them everything—the good, the bad, and the ugly. And then ask them to do the same. When you both share, you will feel the weight lifted off your shoulders. The two of you are on the same team. You win together or lose together. You lean on one another through thick and thin. That's what your marriage commitment is all about. Your hard season may linger but you can make it through when you face it together—hand in hand and heart to heart.

Any kind of hardship can take a toll on your marriage. For example, financial strain, stress at work, frequent travel with work, difficulty with kids, major illness, broken trust, moving, or problems with extended family. These are some common issues that cause husbands and wives to argue or pull away from one another. In the grand scheme of things, the struggles weren't major for Dave and me, but the principles stay the same.

Dave

Hard times are when we need each other the most. And it is

essential to know how to bring peace to any marriage conflict.

Have you ever felt like your marriage was stuck in a cycle of negativity? Ashley and I have. Without meaning to, you and your spouse seem to keep falling back into the same rut of negativity and criticism and you're not sure how to get out of it. I think most (if not all) marriages have experienced this at one time or another.

There are many factors that lead to this negative cycle, which can be set into motion by stress, exhaustion, or mis-communication. How it starts isn't nearly as important as how to break out of it, because if you allow the negative cycle to continue, it can devastate your marriage.

I like to refer to this negative cycle as the *F5 Marriage Tornado*. My knowledge about tornadoes is limited to what I learned from the classic 1990s movie *Twister* (is it just me or were movies way better in the nineties?). I remember the movie teaching that an F5 tornado is the most powerful storm on earth. When you're in the center of an *F5 Marriage Tornado*, it can definitely feel like the most powerful storm in your life.

There are five factors in this storm of marital conflict and they all start with the letter *F* (hence the "F5" reference). Each of these factors leads in a cycle to the next one on the list and with each rotation around all five, the storm grows in ferocity. Maybe you're a visual learner like me, so take a look at this simple graphic explaining the F5 Marriage Tornado.

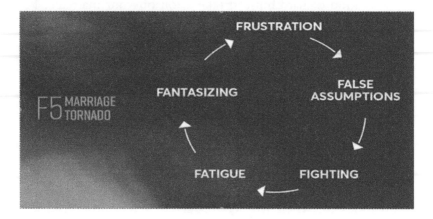

The storm always starts with frustration. We're all prone to frustrations at times and these frustrations might not have anything to do with your spouse, but how you deal with the frustration can have a tremendous impact on how you communicate to your spouse. When you're caught in this storm, frustration always leads to false assumptions.

False assumptions occur when you believe lies that your spouse is against you or they don't care as much as you do about the issue. Once these false assumptions fester, they inevitably lead to fighting which can be a war of words or a war of non-verbal shots aimed at wounding one another.

The fighting eventually leads to fatigue and this is dangerous, because we tend to make our worst decisions when we're tired. Fatigue blurs our vision and keeps us from seeing the situation clearly. Fatigue also makes us susceptible to the fifth step in this cyclone which is fantasizing. When we grow weary from the whole cycle, we can slip into the toxic trap of fantasy in the form of escaping into pornography or romance novels or looking up old flames on social media or just imagining a better life without your spouse.

This process will lead you right back to the start of the storm with more frustration and the cycle continues to repeat itself until one or both spouses either gives up on the marriage or decides to fight for peace.

If you find yourself in this storm that has been the end of far too many marriages, please don't give up. Please don't believe the myth that your marriage will always be caught in this exhausting cycle of negativity and conflict. You have the power to bring peace. The F5 storm has an F5 solution.

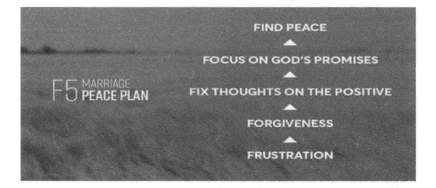

The F5 Peace Plan starts with frustration. Like I said before, frustration is an inevitable part of life and marriage, but you don't have to let that frustration lead you into the storm cycle. In the peace plan, the moment you feel frustration, you break the negative cycle by choosing forgiveness. Choose to let go of whatever grudge or animosity you're carrying. It was Augustine, who centuries ago, wisely said, "Holding a grudge is like drinking poison and then hoping the other person dies."

Grudges and "keeping score" of faults will poison your marriage. Choose to forgive and move forward with grace. This is the first and most important step in finding true and lasting peace in your marriage (and life in general).

After you forgive, follow the Apostle Paul's sage advice recorded in the Bible (Philippians 4:8) and *"fix your thoughts on the good."* Don't let your mind fixate on the negative. Whatever captures your focus will seem bigger, so make sure you're focusing on good things. If you're looking for your spouse's flaws, that's all you'll see, but if you're looking for the good, you'll start to see it.

Fixing your thoughts on the positive should be a constant reminder to proceed to the next step, which is to focus on God's promises. Remember that God is with you and He is bigger than whatever struggle you're facing. His promises are true and can be trusted. Immerse yourself in God's Word (the Bible) and choose to trust that God is in control even when life is difficult.

As you do these things, you'll discover a mental and spiritual renewal, which leads to the final step, which is finding peace. I believe that real peace is found in the Prince of Peace. When Christ is the center of your thoughts, He will always bring more peace to your perspective. He wants to bring more peace to your heart, your home, and your marriage.

I love this simple peace plan for many reasons, but one of the most practical reasons is that you don't need your spouse to participate with you to do it. You don't have to get stuck in the cynical cycle of excuses that says, *Well if my husband/wife would just do their part, then the marriage would be great.* It's never your job to fix your spouse or change your spouse. It's your job to love your spouse and to trust God to do the rest.

If you will follow this peace plan, even if your spouse isn't currently joining you in the peace process, you'll still find that God will start bringing more peace to your home. I believe your example will eventually be a factor in bringing a change of heart to your spouse too.

Choose to be the first one to stop the fighting. Refuse to keep living in the eye of an *F5 Marriage Tornado* when peace is within your grasp. Trust the Prince of Peace to calm the storms and He will. You're on the same team so you will either win together or lose together.

Ashley

There are major issues that a married couple must work through that are worth hashing out in a healthy and respectful manner, but there are also minor, preferential things that we honestly will just have to let go so we can pursue peace *over* pride.

Dave and I get along well for the most part, but there is one subject that has tripped us up and made us argue a lot in recent years. That subject is the real estate website called Zillow.com. I know, I know, this seems utterly ridiculous, right? Well, let me explain. Dave and I are both fans of Zillow because it makes browsing houses for sale easy, and it also includes a lot of information on the homes and neighborhoods, including a little figure they call the "Zestimate." This number is Zillow's estimate of what your house is worth based on an algorithm that takes into account recent home sales in your general area. However, any real estate agent out there will tell you that the Zestimate isn't always correct because it doesn't look at the real estate market as a whole.

Over the years, Dave has looked at the Zestimate for our home just in case we needed to sell, and almost every time he would get upset because he felt like the Zestimate was rather low. Then, he would say things like, "Sweetie, we're just not going to be able to sell this home for what we thought we could sell it for because *everybody* looks at the Zestimate." Then, I would tell him that the Zestimate isn't always right and that our house is worth more. Then he would get upset with me because he felt like I wasn't taking the Zestimate seriously enough. Friends, we would have this ridiculous back-and-forth bickering about a silly algorithm. Yeah.

Eventually, we both realized that arguing over the Zestimate was getting us nowhere, and honestly, it just wasn't worth it. Our relationship was and still is more important. So, we decided that we wouldn't talk about Zillow or the Zestimate anymore and we both couldn't be happier about it—*a minor issue.*

Taking Turns

Dave and I have a lot in common, but this doesn't necessarily ring true when it comes to television shows. In the beginning of our marriage, deciding which show we were going to watch was a source of tension. As one who lives in a home full of boys, I love to watch the girly-est shows possible like *Gilmore Girls*, *Say Yes to the Dress*, and *Four Weddings* when I have the remote. Dave, however, could not care less about these, even though he has graciously watched a few of them with me on more than one occasion.

So, what's a couple to do when you can't agree on what to watch? We do what we tell our *kids* to do. We take turns. We try and engage in what our spouse likes to watch, and we share our favorite shows with him/her too.

For Dave and me, this has been fun. We've found some shows we can enjoy together, but we try to take turns watching some of our individual favorites too. Just recently, the NFL Draft was on and I knew Dave wanted to watch it. He didn't ask, but I went ahead and turned to that channel. I loved seeing his face light up. As I watched it with him, I asked him questions about how the NFL Draft works and honestly, I really enjoyed it. Now I know a thing or two about it that I didn't know before—which was nothing at all. Gotta start somewhere, right?

So, get in there. Take turns, or better yet, turn off the television and go for a walk together. Fighting over television shows just isn't worth it. I love what Romans 12:18 says:

"If it is possible, as far as it depends on you, live at peace with everyone"
(NIV).

Television isn't the only source of tension for couples. I've talked to many couples who fight about how to *properly* load the dishwasher. One feels strongly that the dishes must be *pre-cleaned* before placing them neatly in the dishwasher, while the other crams every dish possible in the dishwasher and hopes it will clean them efficiently. I get it. Both sides have a point, but this issue isn't worth fighting over.

So, what's a couple to do? If you feel strongly about the dishwasher being super organized and all dishes being pre-washed by hand, then do it that way. Don't make your spouse feel like he/she is a slob because they don't follow your exact method. You can kindly give him/her some pointers, but it's not worth fighting over.

In the end, how the dishes are arranged and cleaned doesn't really matter. So, make peace with one another in this area, and stop fighting about it. Let it go. You'll feel so much freedom, and you'll still have clean dishes at the end of the day.

"Peacemakers who sow in peace reap a harvest of righteousness"
James 3:18 (NIV)

Cuddle Bug

Another source of tension that Dave and I faced early in our marriage was *to cuddle or not to cuddle*. All you "cuddlers" out there are excited about this one, aren't you? Married people *should* cuddle from time to time, but the frequency and cuddle-style can greatly differ from person to person. This discrepancy caused a few arguments for Dave and me in the beginning of our marriage, but this is one of those things that will take some compromise from both spouses. Those who are more affectionate may need a little more cuddle time, but too much cuddling can wear on those who feel suffocated by it.

For example, in our home Dave is the *cuddler*. I like some cuddling, but prolonged cuddling feels too binding to me. Crazy, right? But I know I'm not alone in this sentiment. I can't cuddle all night long because I move a lot when I sleep. So, what do we do? We meet in the middle. I cuddle some with Dave before we go to bed, and then he gives me the space that I need to go to sleep. It's honestly become this big joke between us, but we both have our needs met without any tension between us and this helps us to avoid the "F5" cycle. But more than anything, we want to express God's love to one another.

"But the fruit of the Spirit is love, joy, peace, forbearance, kindness, goodness, faithfulness"
Galatians 5:22 (NLT)

Let It Go

There are some of us—*ahem*, me included—who like order. We like our clothes, towels, and linens folded a specific way, and when they are not, it drives us bonkers. And, we let our spouse know it—only to cause more frustration in our marriage. It's just not worth it. They are pieces of fabric, for crying out loud! Our life will not fall apart if everything isn't folded the exact same way.

So, what should we do? If how the clothes and towels are folded means a lot to you, then kindly show your spouse how you prefer it done. If they don't get it exactly right every time, don't lay into them about it. Just go back and refold it when they aren't in the room or learn to shake it off and appreciate that the garment/towel is folded and put away at all. It's all about choosing peace over perfection. Let's let go of the petty stuff and focus on the important things. Let's make a conscious effort to choose peace over perfection every day.

"The Lord gives strength to his people; the Lord blesses his people with peace"
Psalm 29:11 (NIV)

This is a silly one, but so many times couples end up fighting over what temperature a space should be. Silly right? Sometimes the biggest fights are over the smallest matters. We all want our homes (and even our cars) to be comfortable, but we usually have a different "ideal temperature" than our spouse. We end up fighting over how hot or cold our house or car needs to be. How silly is that?

Dave and I used to disagree over this, but we've found a way to compromise. I like our spaces to be really cold. At night, I lower the thermostat and even turn on the ceiling fan, and Dave bundles up next to me. We've learned that we can both have what we want in this situation, and the temperature of our home is simply not worth the fight.

"Let us therefore make every effort to do what leads to peace and to mutual edification"
Romans 14:19 (NIV)

Do you and your spouse struggle with any of these things? If so, talk about it and let today be the day that you both make peace with one another and collectively decide to stop fighting over these unimportant things. You'll be so glad you did and the two of you will enjoy a much happier and healthier marriage and home.

Dave

When God created the concept of marriage, He simultaneously gave us an extraordinary gift *and* an extraordinary challenge. Marriage requires an unshakable commitment to one another even when your spouse is intimately aware of your flaws. 1 Corinthians 13:4–8a reminds us,

> *"Love is patient and kind; love does not envy or boast; it is not arrogant or rude. It does not insist on its own way; it is not irritable or resentful; it does not rejoice at wrongdoing but rejoices with the truth. Love bears all things, believes all things, hopes all things, endures all things. Love never ends."*
> *(ESV)*

These famous words aren't just a poetic description of love; they are a practical road map to guide your marriage in the right direction through hardships and conflict. Be patient and kind to your spouse and refuse to allow the poison of pride to taint your marriage. One way to end conflict is by choosing to put your spouse's needs ahead of your own. Ephesians 4:26b reads,

> *"Don't let the sun go down on your anger"*
> *(ESV)*.

We do this by not allowing space for spite or hostility in our marriages. Instead, allow grace and forgiveness to flow freely to your spouse, and refuse to deceive or keep secrets from one another.

Finally, make a conscious decision to love one another using God's definition of love. Allow love to lead your marriage, and you will always overcome any hardship that you face. And most of all, God is for your marriage, so never give up on one another!

4

NAKED SEX

Dave

My mom and dad were kind of freaks when I was growing up. Okay. They were the sweetest Christian couple, but they were like *Fifty Shades of Middle Age*! They were all over each other, which was gross as a kid, but truthfully it made me excited to be married one day, because I knew I wanted the same thing. My mom is the sweetest woman I know—picture a fashionable Mother Teresa and that's my mom—but I was terrified for Ashley to meet my parents for the first time. Let's just say they were very comfortable letting everyone know they were *happily* married and that their passion for each other was burning bright.

For example, we met at a restaurant the first time I introduced Mom and Dad to Ashley and my mom went up to Ashley and said, "Oh my goodness, you are just so pretty," as she patted Ashley's cheek and continued, "I'm just so excited to meet you. Oh, here—let's just sit down so we can get to know each other." And as she and Ashley are sitting down she said, "Oh my bottom!" I'm standing there wondering what in the world is happening. And then she said, "You are probably wondering why my bottom is sore?" I was in shock thinking, *No! No! We aren't wondering why your bottom is hurting! Stop!* And then she started telling this story that I didn't want to hear, but I was fighting my gag reflex, so I couldn't get any words out and stop her!

Then, she said, "Well, before we came here, I had just

gotten out of the shower when David's father, Brad, started *tantalizing* me, and he was chasing me around the bathroom trying to spank me with my curling iron. I was trying to get him to stop, telling him (teasingly) *no, no, stop it Brad, stop it! It's hot!* Brad thought "hot" meant exciting, but I was actually trying to get him to realize that the curling iron was hot because I had turned it on and was going to use it, but then he spanked me with it on my bare bottom and he singed me. So, my bottom is a little bit sore—so what are you going to have for lunch?"

Nothing! Is what I was thinking.

I had completely lost my appetite!

Ashley

Dave and I can laugh about this story now, but that was his upbringing and my first encounter with his parents. As a kid, he was blessed to have his parents model sex as being good and fun. My parents love each other and are very close and committed to each other, but growing up they were rarely affectionate around me or anyone else in public. The subject of sex really wasn't something we talked about as a family, and whenever it happened to pop up in conversation, my parents would try to change the subject or say something derogatory about the act to make it seem as unappealing as possible. Looking back, I know my parents were just trying to keep me chaste, and they weren't sure how to talk about sex without having to address their own pasts or answer awkward questions. I think this is true for a lot of people growing up.

How do we have the kind of sex life that God wants us to have when we both come into the marriage with different perspectives about how things are supposed to be? Well, a great place to start is us striving to meet each other's sexual needs.

The Bible gives us a road map when it comes to sex in 1 Corinthians 7:3–4:

"The husband should fulfill his marital duty to his wife, and likewise the wife to her husband. The wife does not have authority over her own body but yields it to her husband. In the same way, the husband does not have authority over his own body but yields it to his wife."
(NIV)

In other words, it's all about serving each other's needs. When it comes to sex, spouses are the only legitimate means to fulfill one another's sexual appetites. Sex is a gift from God that is exclusively for married couples, and we should do our very best to cultivate a thriving sex life with our spouse by talking openly and honestly about it with them and by having it often.

Captivating

The strongest marriages have a husband who continuously pursues his wife, and a wife who continuously affirms her husband. This is something that I think we are really good at doing when we are first dating and when we are engaged or during the first year of marriage, but then it starts to fizzle out the longer we are married, and we can start to lose that spark. Friends, we need to stoke the fire and keep it burning! Husbands, your wife wants to know that you find her absolutely captivating. And ladies, your husband wants to know that you think he is capable—that he is the man!

Again, couples who have the best sex life have a man who continuously pursues, romances, and adores his wife and a wife who continuously affirms her husband and who shows her respect and belief in him. This helps both the husband and the wife to be at their best. Proverbs 5:18–19 reads,

"Let your wife be a fountain of blessing for you. Rejoice in the wife of your youth. She is a loving deer, a graceful doe. Let her breasts satisfy you always. May you always be captivated by her love."
(NLT)

This is a beautiful picture of how a couple shares their passion with one another. Our marriages are strong when we choose to passionately pursue and affirm one another and when we make sex a priority.

God created sex. Think about that for a second! Maybe you've had some common-but-misguided views of God where He is cold or distant or out of touch, and He's looking down on anybody who's having a good time. When you think about sex, you might visualize God shaking His head in disappointment or disgust, but *He's* the one who thought of it first! Everything good in the world is something God thought of first. We believe that sex is one of God's most awesome creations.

Dave

God in all His wisdom could've been fine without making the human race in the first place. Even after making mankind, He could have made us asexual beings that just spawned more humans without needing any sex at all. But He chose to create sex. He chose to make it pleasurable.

Perhaps one of the reasons why we get uneasy talking about sexuality is because sex isn't always a positive experience. Sex is certainly a wonderful gift, but sometimes it gets misused, misplaced or misunderstood. When that happens, emotional pain replaces physical pleasure and baggage finds its way into the bedroom. Whether we realize it or not, we all have some form of baggage related to sex.

Laying Down the Burdens

Some of our sexual baggage has to do with past regrets. When we've made sexual choices that were out of bounds from God's original and perfect design for sex, it creates a visual reel in our brains full of images we wish we could erase. Sometimes our sexual baggage comes from being raised with an unhealthy view of sex that misrepresented what sexual intimacy was all about and it created misguided views or unrealistic expectations.

Some of us have sexual baggage because of past abuse. These wounds can be the deepest and most painful of them all. A staggering number of people have been abused, molested, objectified, or mistreated in a way that leaves deep scars. Sex was never intended to be used as a weapon to hurt others or as a lust-fueled form of self-gratification at the expense of others. Lust sees people as objects to be used and exploited. But love sees people as souls to be cherished and respected.

So many of us are carrying scars because of these intimate and invisible wounds. Whether the wounds came from our own choices or from becoming the victim of someone else's choices, these wounds can seep into a marriage and cause distrust, disunity, and discouragement. If you're currently struggling to connect with your spouse inside and/or outside the bedroom, please know that things can get better. And this happens when both the husband and the wife make sexual intimacy and fulfillment a high priority in the marriage. Each spouse should put the other spouse's needs ahead of his or her own needs. This mutual selflessness is the key to a great sex life, but it's also the key to a great marriage outside the bedroom.

Ashley

I love this verse about sex,

> "Kiss me and kiss me again! Your love is sweeter than wine."
> Song of Solomon 1:2 (NLT).

Friends, this is the Bible, but somewhere along the line, people started believing a lie that God doesn't like sex and He especially doesn't want us to enjoy it. Nothing could be further from the truth! Sex is a powerful gift and when enjoyed within a committed marriage, it should be passionate and pleasurable. Just read the book of the Song of Solomon in the Bible, which is essentially erotic love poetry. It is pretty steamy! God wants us to have this kind of passionate, playful intimacy within our marriages, too.

Genesis 2:25 reads,

"Now the man and his wife were both naked, but they felt no shame."
(NLT)

The first picture of sex and marriage the Bible paints for us tells us that the couple was naked but felt no shame. This is a beautiful image of the vulnerability, trust, honesty, transparency, and intimacy that should create a healthy foundation for every marriage. God wants a husband and wife to be *naked* physically, spiritually, and emotionally with one another. When you have a *naked marriage* with no secrets and total vulnerability, you can experience true and lasting intimacy without shame or fear. Sex isn't just a physical act—it's a sacred, spiritual one as well.

Dave

What happens when we forget or haven't been taught that sex is sacred? We get burned. When we reduce sex only to an act of physical pleasure, we're *using* our partner instead of truly loving him/her. Sex is supposed to deepen our love for one another, not hinder it. We're creating a bond with our spouse that goes far beyond the physical. "Do you not know that your bodies are members of Christ himself? Shall I then take the members of Christ and unite them with a prostitute? Never! Do you not know that he who unites himself with a prostitute is one with her in body? For it is said,

> *'The two will become one flesh.' But whoever is united with the Lord is one with him in spirit."*
> 1 Corinthians 6:15–17 (NIV)

Sex is meant to be binding. This is why there is so much pain, confusion, and heartbreak involved in broken relationships with sexual partners that don't exist with other kinds of relationships.

Lifelong monogamy within marriage was and still is God's plan for sex. God wants your sex life to be amazing, but it needs to be amazing with the person you married. If you start looking outside the marriage, then everybody gets hurt. Think of sex like fire, and marriage like a fireplace. When fire stays in the fireplace it gives off light and warmth to the entire house, but when you take fire out of the fireplace and spread it around to other places, everyone gets burned! So, do your best to keep the fire burning bright in *your* fireplace, and make sex a priority in your marriage.

Chore-Play

Recently, I was eating lunch with a friend when he shared some frustrations: "What am I supposed to do if my wife won't have sex with me?"

I wasn't surprised by the bluntness of his question. Having worked with married couples for many years, I've heard it all (or at least I've heard a lot). His frustration is a relatively common one and this area of "sexual neglect" is one of the most frustrating marriage issues I hear from husbands (and in some cases from wives as well).

My friend went on to unpack more of his marital history. He told me that the marriage started off well, and in the early stages of their relationship there had been a healthy sex life.

Both spouses seemed satisfied by the level of frequency and intimacy in their bedroom. But now, their marriage bed seemed to be a cold and uninviting place where both spouses curled up on their own side with no physical touch at all.

At some point, there seemed to be a change in his wife's sex drive. He couldn't pinpoint a certain time or event where things changed, but for years there had been a noticeable downward trajectory in their sexual intimacy. He had done all he knew to do to turn the tide. He had tried to meet her needs. He had communicated about his own needs. He had lost all dignity and downright begged and pleaded, but he felt like he was a starving man being forced to live on dwindling crumbs, in a sexless marriage.

My friend was feeling a mixture of negative emotions. He felt betrayed. He believed his wife's withholding of sex was equal to an act of infidelity since she was refusing one of her basic "duties" as a spouse. He also felt abandoned and rejected, because his bride was seemingly giving him the cold shoulder. He was sad, hurt, frustrated, confused, and angry. He wasn't sure what to do next. His anger was beginning to devolve into apathy toward his wife, which can be the final kiss of death before divorce.

Experience has taught me that most marriages will face seasons where one or both spouses feel a certain amount of sexual neglect. If left unchecked, this season can morph into a new reality where it's difficult to find a restart and the marriage can tragically end in either a divorce or a life of disgruntled coexisting—without true love or partnership.

I encouraged my friend to commit to a season of selflessly serving his spouse and asking nothing in return. Since this is a common issue for husbands, I tell them to learn their wife's "love language" and speak it fluently. Serve her, and not with a cold-hearted sense of entitlement. Serve her selflessly as Christ loved and served His bride (the church) giving Himself up for her. Let your tenderness be evident in your words and your actions. Which means, speak with a loving *tone*. Consider the act of loving and serving her a privilege, regardless of whether she may eventually reciprocate.

Look for ways to reconnect outside the bedroom. To reverse the drift that's happening between you and her, don't put your focus on reconnecting in the bedroom. Putting so much pressure on the act of sex itself will potentially push your wife even further away. You need "foreplay." Look for ways to laugh together. Create new adventures together. Start dating each other again if date nights are something that has stopped happening. Make conversation a priority. Pursue her and win her heart all over again. Let her know you are thinking about her all day long.

Foreplay doesn't begin five minutes before you're hoping to get it on. It should begin the moment you wake up in the morning. Every text message, every hug, every act of service, every phone call, every wink, every kiss, every "I love you," and every interaction with each other is an opportunity to make a connection that could rebuild your connection.

Also, men, if you want to get your wife in the mood, try "Chore-Play." Do the dishes or fold some laundry. Most men are visual. Seeing their wife in lingerie is enough to instantly get in the mood. Most women are more complex in their process of becoming aroused. Sure, ladies want their man to look his best, but she also wants her mental to-do list to be clear so she can focus. Guys, you can help her get in the mindset by doing some household chores. You'll never look hotter in her eyes than when she catches you doing the dishes or folding some laundry!

Guys, don't give up. Don't quit on each other. Keep fighting for each other and not against each other. Keep pursuing paths to healing and connection. Don't blame each other. Don't assume the worst of each other. Choose to believe the best in your spouse and choose to trust that God will carry you through this. Your best days are ahead if you don't give up.

Ashley

We know that sex is important, and that God created it to be enjoyed and celebrated in marriage, but what happens when you just aren't *feeling* sexy? Now ladies, I know you can all relate to me on this. Sometimes after having babies or just not looking the way we did when we first got married, it can be hard to feel sexy or to feel like we are desirable to our spouse.

Not too long ago some girl friends and I started talking about our marriages over lunch. One of my friends shared that she feels like her husband is never satisfied with the frequency of their sex life, and she is frustrated because she feels insecure with her body.

"I mean, I've had a bunch of kids. I don't look anything like I did when we were first married. I just don't feel sexy."

The more we talked, the more the women in our group agreed that they also deal with a lot of insecurity with their bodies.

Can you relate? I certainly can. There have definitely been times when I've felt pudgy and unattractive, and sex was honestly the last thing on my brain. So, I get it. However, the truth is that the less often we have sex with our spouse, the less desire we have for sex. And we fall into a terrible cycle of having little to no sex and both spouses find themselves extremely frustrated and even bitter toward one another. That's why it's important that we do our best to overcome these body issues and work to cultivate and maintain a great sex life with our husband. Here are some practical ways to do that.

As women, we need to embrace our body as it is currently—not stressing over our imaginary *ideal body*. This is hard, but it is a game-changer when it comes to enjoying sex. We can't fully engage in sex and be worrying about our stretch marks or cellulite at the same time. In fact, it totally stresses us out! And stress makes us feel tired and unmotivated to do anything—especially sex!

De-stressing

The stress we feel when we obsess about our body not being what we think it should be ends up killing our desire for sex altogether. We need to intentionally shift our thoughts. The next time personal body-shaming thoughts start to fill our mind, we must "shut them down" and replace them with positive thoughts. For example, let's see our few extra pounds as curves instead of cellulite. Odds are your husband really loves those curves anyway. As women, we tend to hold ourselves to crazy standards based on airbrushed, photoshopped models who don't even exist. Ladies, let's stop torturing ourselves and embrace the body that we have now! Let's choose to love ourselves. There is nothing sexier than confidence, and this confidence and intentional self-acceptance will help us to de-stress and be more in the mood for romance.

Another great marriage builder is to start having sex more often with your husband. At a recent conference, a friend of ours shared that she had extreme anxiety about having sex with her husband after having their first child. She felt exhausted and totally insecure about her "mom-bod" to the point that she dreaded the day when the postpartum six-week waiting period was up and she and her husband could make love once again. When the day arrived, her husband was patient with her, but she completely froze up and all she could do was cry. Weeks went by. A month passed, and her husband patiently waited.

She could feel a distance growing between them, even though her husband was being so understanding and tender with her. Eventually, she realized that she had to do something.

When she shared her predicament with a close friend, her friend looked in her eyes and plainly said, "You need to have sex with your husband today. Stop dreading this day and just go for it, or you'll just keep feeling anxious about it and frustrate him to no end." My friend knew that this was the truth she needed to hear and live out. She went to her husband, and they made love. Then, they did it the next day and the next. As my friend recalled this story, she said that something happened that she never expected. The more she and her husband made love, the more her desire for sex increased and her anxiety subsided.

Friends, sometimes we just need to go for it, regardless of our hang-ups. This doesn't mean that we discount our feelings or our husband's feelings. Sometimes, we may be facing deeper issues that we need to address with a Christian counselor or doctor. Whatever the circumstance, we should be willing to do whatever it takes to get to the root of why we aren't having sex, and we should do our best to make sex a priority in our marriage. The more often we make love with our spouse, the more we will want it and the less stressed we will be.

Sexy Investment

I also think we women should invest in some sexy lingerie. I used to think that lingerie was kind of ridiculous because the whole point of wearing it was for it to end up on the floor. Right? But over the years, I've seen what a turn-on it can be for both husbands and wives. Most men love for their wives to wear lingerie because they see it as sexy gift-wrapping with all the lace and bows. And for most women, the very act of wearing lingerie can make them feel sexy and in the mood. You don't have to spend a lot of money or get something uncomfortable. In fact, there are so many styles and sizes available these days. So, give it try. Go shopping for a pretty bra and lacy panties and surprise your husband with your findings when he gets home. You'll be surprised at how sexy you'll feel, and your husband will love it!

Bottom line, we all have insecurities about our bodies, but we can choose whether we allow these insecurities to negatively impact our sex life and marriage. Ladies, let's choose to overcome. Let's choose to see our bodies as beautiful and sexy just as they are. Let's choose to be confident and make sex a priority in our marriage. When we do this, we will enjoy a thriving sex life and a stronger, more connected marriage.

Dave

We all have some level of insecurity. Being in perfect physical shape isn't the solution (although better overall health can be a positive factor); the real issues are deeper than the surface. I think it is important to remember what it means to have a "naked and unashamed" marriage.

Our first picture of the first married couple in the Bible's Book of Genesis tells us that Adam and Eve were "naked and unashamed." I'm sure they were in good shape, but they weren't "naked and perfect." There were no other humans around to compare themselves to. It wasn't about comparison. It wasn't about looking in the mirror (because mirrors didn't exist).

They had a beautiful connection and intimacy because they were focused on each other's souls, not each other's physical imperfections. Find the courage and vulnerability to be "naked and unashamed." It will take time, but it will create such comfort, security, and intimacy in your marriage bed (and every other part of your marriage too).

I know you might feel uncomfortable being seen, but your spouse wants to see you while you're making love. Especially for men, most guys are wired up to be more engaged and connected to their wife through visual stimulus. You might not want to see yourself, but he wants to see you! If having all the lights on seems too intimidating, start with candlelight. The soft light is flattering to the figure and it also sets a romantic tone that could make you both feel more comfortable.

When we have physical insecurities, it starts a domino effect. You don't feel sexy, so you don't want to think about sex, and you get uncomfortable when your spouse initiates sex. Then your spouse gets hurt feelings and the marriage gets stuck in a negative cycle of perpetual frustration and miscommunication. If this is accurately describing the current dynamics in your marriage, then you need to rewire your thinking. Confidence is not just a feeling. You might not feel confident about yourself right now, but you can choose to project confidence and before long, you'll start feeling it. I'm not making this up! There's plenty of research out there to back this up. There's nothing sexier than confidence.

Ashley

I often receive messages from wives who are frustrated with the physical intimacy in their marriage. They love their husbands and want to make sex a priority, but they have a hard time getting "in the mood." Between work, kids, household duties, extracurricular activities, homework, church, and everything else, it can be difficult to shut down the ever-increasing mental clutter in our minds. Sadly, sex often becomes just another item on the "to-do" list. When we see sex from this perspective, we start resenting it and miss out on the incredible gift that God designed it to be for a husband and wife. So, how can we break this negative cycle?

Just as we must clean out, manage, and organize the physical clutter in our homes and offices, we must similarly approach our mental clutter. First, get rid of the negative thoughts that are preventing you from fully embracing sex with your husband. According to the Bible, we can do this by taking our thoughts captive. 2 Corinthians 10:5 reads,

> *"We demolish arguments and every pretension that sets itself up against the knowledge of God, and we take captive every thought to make it obedient to Christ."*
> *(NIV)*

This is important when it comes to our mental clutter.

When we feel exhausted and overwhelmed by the idea that we need to have sex with our husband in addition to everything else on our to-do list, we end up arguing with one another. This frustrates our relationship. Take a step back and recognize the thought processes that shut you down when it comes to sex. What tasks or negative thoughts tend to be at the forefront of your mind? It might help to journal about these questions to help pinpoint the issues. Sometimes putting pen to paper helps sort out and even organize our thoughts more effectively. Once you pinpoint the problems, recognize the negative thoughts as they come and choose to approach sex more positively.

Regardless of our specific hang-ups, we must realize that sex is a gift from the Lord, and it is a privilege for a husband and wife to be the only legitimate means to meet this God-given need. So, when thoughts like *I don't have time for sex tonight*, or *I'm too tired for sex tonight*, or *Really? Didn't we just do it yesterday?* come to the forefront of your mind, stop these thoughts in their tracks and replace them with the truth. Remember, sex is a healthy desire and gift from the Lord meant explicitly for marriage. It's also true that regularly having sex brings a married couple closer together—relieving stress. And having sex with your husband and investing in your marriage is more important than folding laundry or packing school lunches right at that moment.

Anxious Thoughts

Sometimes the pressure that we feel isn't from a to-do list at all. This kind of mental clutter goes much deeper. Things like fear, worry, and insecurity can take up so much of our mental energy that we have very little left to give our husband—especially when it comes to sex and romance. And the longer you go without making love with your spouse, the more pressure and even awkwardness you will feel. Unfortunately, the problem only gets worse. Instead of allowing these thoughts to hold you down, be honest with your husband about how you are feeling and be willing to seek help.

When we reject our husband's advances or snap at him for wanting to make love, we can make him feel like we don't desire him, love him, or respect him. However, when we open up and have a conversation with him about our fears, insecurities, and worries, we prepare the path of intimacy. And we give him an opportunity to join us in prayer and offer us some perspective, support, and encouragement.

If the worrisome thoughts become something you experience every day and are causing you great anxiety and resentment when it comes to sex, it might be time to seek the help of a professional counselor. A Christian counselor helps people to recognize the anxious thoughts that are holding them back and aids them in understanding how to replace these anxious thoughts with God's healing truth. You can find a list of Christian counselors near you by contacting your local church.

The most important thing we must remember when it comes to anxious thoughts is that we can't expect them just to go away. The more we pray and ask God to replace these thoughts with His truth, and the more we open up about our feelings with our husband and counselor, the more freedom we will have from this anxious mental clutter. And, over time, we will have the peace of mind and balance that we so desire, as we cultivate a thriving intimate life and marriage.

Dave

A friend recently shared some frustrations with me about his "boring sex life." I thought he might complain about a lack of frequency (which is the most common complaint I hear from sexually frustrated spouses), but that wasn't his grievance. He launched into a frustrated tirade as if his feelings had been bottled up for years.

He said, "When we first got together, there were no limits in our sex life. My wife was ready to act out any fantasy I could imagine. Both of us had a wild past and our views of sex were shaped by our own experiences and a lot of exposure to porn. We even watched a lot of porn together as a way to spice things up. Our relationship wasn't great, but our sex life was amazing.

"When we got serious about our faith, we realized that porn was 'out of bounds' in a Christian marriage. Jesus taught that to look at another person with lust is to commit adultery in your heart. It was tough to give up, but we both felt like it was the right thing. The problem now is that while our marriage is better overall, our sex life feels like it's at an all-time low."

I asked him to elaborate and *what he said next surprised me*...He said, "Porn taught me certain things about sex. We used to do those things and she doesn't want to do them anymore." I didn't ask for specifics, but I was pretty sure he was talking about oral sex and/or anal sex which are both acted out in pornography with as much frequency as vaginal intercourse. I know this from my own past struggles with pornography.

He said, "Because she's not willing to do 'it' anymore, I feel like she doesn't want to give all of herself to me in the same way she used to. Even though she has given herself in the same way to many other men in her past. I mean, I'm her husband and she's giving me less than she gave to random men she hooked up with before we were together."

As my friend continued to process these complicated thoughts and feelings, I began to realize that his frustration with his sex life wasn't just the lack of a specific physical act; it had an emotional aspect to it as well. Sex is never just a physical act. Her preference to stop doing certain things in bed was causing him mental and emotional torment.

He was picturing his wife giving "all of herself" to other men in her past in a way that she was not willing to give to him. It was like she was saying those other men in her past were more worthy of her uninhibited sexuality than he was. He wasn't just feeling sexually frustrated, he was feeling rejected and disconnected from his wife.

He asked with frustration in his voice, "Other than hurting each other or bringing someone else into the act, I don't think anything should be 'off-limits' in the bedroom for a husband and a wife! Am I wrong?"

I weighed carefully what I said next, because I knew that this situation was complex. I also knew that many people face these same struggles of feeling bored in the bedroom, but no two situations are exactly alike. I believe that God gives an enormous amount of freedom in the marriage bed and wants us to have a thriving and passionate sex life. But if I simply validated my friend's feelings and frustrations, I could ultimately hurt his marriage by fueling his sense of entitlement. I didn't want my friend to leave our lunch only to make selfish demands of his wife instead of making the necessary effort to love and serve her with tenderness and selflessness.

I told him that he needed to talk openly about these issues with his wife. But not just in a demanding way, trying to coerce her into following his specific desires. I told him that by withholding certain sexual acts, his wife wasn't trying to deprive him or give less of herself to him, but to actually give more of herself to him. He looked really confused by that, so I elaborated further.

I said that his wife had probably come to associate certain sexual acts as part of her painful and promiscuous past, full of brokenness and regret. For her, certain acts might remind her of baggage that she wants to let go. The memories of her past made her feel dirty, defiled, and devalued. She is forgiven of her past and the Bible describes her as a new creation in Christ. She wanted to give her best to her husband as a pure bride, but it made him feel like she was a prude. If God really created sex and wanted it to be at its best within marriage, then why were they both so frustrated?

I told my friend that this (like most issues in marriage) wasn't about who was "right" and who was "wrong." This issue was about both spouses communicating with transparency and expressing their feelings with vulnerability. It was about striving to serve each other's needs with selflessness, thoughtfulness, mutual respect, and love. The goal was to find a solution that strengthened their marriage. If they both would approach the conversation without demands, but with a desire to truly understand each other, they'd be off to the right start.

Every couple must deal with issues in the bedroom. Your sexual intimacy can and *should* be one of the most fulfilling and *fun* aspects of your marriage, but it won't happen automatically. Both you and your spouse have baggage, expectations, hangups, hurts, and a myriad of other factors that need to be communicated for both of you to experience physical pleasure, emotional intimacy, and the spiritual oneness that God intends to happen whenever a husband and wife make love.

Ashley

In our work with married couples, Dave and I have found that most couples won't (or don't know how to) have these important conversations. It feels too vulnerable or scary. Perhaps they just don't know how to put words to what they're feeling without making demands or accusations. But deeper connection always begins with communication. When you improve your communication, you'll improve your sex life, but you'll also simultaneously improve every other aspect of your relationship! We know these issues can be uncomfortable to talk about, but they're vitally important. As husband and wife, you should be able to talk about anything. Get naked (both physically and emotionally). Get vulnerable. Put your spouse's needs ahead of your own. It will do wonders to help you both grow deeper in your intimacy both inside and outside the bedroom.

What's Normal?

When we got married, Dave and I had saved ourselves for each other. This wasn't easy, nor were we perfect in every way, but we made it to the wedding day without having sex. I was so excited about the wedding night, but also extremely nervous, as you can imagine. Needless to say, it was great, but it took some getting used to. I really liked it, but Dave *loved* it. The more I have talked and counseled other married couples, the more I have found that this is pretty common. There is usually one spouse that has a greater need for sex. And that's okay.

I didn't realize this truth as a newlywed, and it gave me a lot of anxiety. I started to think something was wrong with me. Why didn't I want to do it as much as Dave? How many times a week was normal? And so on. My anxiety certainly didn't help my desire, if you know what I mean. It was awkward for a while, but then I read a book called *His Needs, Her Needs*, by Willard F. Harley, and it all clicked for me. Harley explained that in most marriages there is usually one partner who has a stronger need for sex and will want to have it more frequently. He also said that the couple should try to aim to have sex as often as possible to fulfill this need and protect the marriage.

I love how *The Message* paraphrases 1 Corinthians 7:3-4:

> *"It's good for a man to have a wife, and for a woman to have a husband. Sexual drives are strong, but marriage is strong enough to contain them and provide for a balanced and fulfilling sexual life in a world of sexual disorder. The marriage bed must be a place of mutuality—the husband seeking to satisfy his wife, the wife seeking to satisfy her husband. Marriage is not a place to "stand up for your rights."*

Marriage is a decision to serve the other, whether in bed or out. Abstaining from sex is permissible for a period of time if you both agree to it, and if it's for the purposes of prayer and fasting—but only for such times. Then come back together again. Satan has an ingenious way of tempting us when we least expect it. I'm not, understand, commanding these periods of abstinence—only providing my best counsel if you should choose them.

There is so much at stake: our marital intimacy, our sexual health, and most importantly, our commitment to the one we love most. We must strive to get this right. God designed sex specifically for marriage. He wants us to have a healthy, enjoyable and thriving sex life with our spouse. Let's not withhold this sacred act of love and service from each other!

More than Friends!

Friendship is the fertile soil in which a healthy sex life can grow and thrive. Cultivating your friendship with your spouse will also help you both to create a vibrant sex life. However, it takes time and intentionality to foster an ongoing friendship with our spouse. When we first get married, we're thinking, *No problem! My spouse and I are best friends!* But as time goes on, we can start to drift apart because life is busy, and we are raising kids or just dealing with the daily stresses of life. Friendship takes time and constant focus. Practically speaking, how do we do this?

For Dave and me, our best days are days we go on a walk and hold hands. Or, at the end of the day, Dave will rub my feet while we talk, and this helps us to daily feel connected to each other. Truthfully, guys, the nonsexual touch is huge for your wife and for cultivating intimacy with her. Along with "Chore-Play," nonsexual touch and open communication throughout the day is the *best* foreplay for your wife.

Husbands, I just want to give you a tip—women feel more inclined to have sex with their husbands when they feel connected to them emotionally and intellectually. This happens through communication. So, guys, if you feel like your wife is just never in the mood for sex, then I would ask you, *When is the last time you had a heart-to-heart conversation? When is the last time you gave her nonsexual touch and you really listened to her and you really shared your heart with her?* because this is how intimacy starts for a woman and what eventually leads her to the bedroom.

When it comes to sex, a woman's emotional state directly affects her sex drive. We want to feel close to our husbands before we become intimate with them. We can't argue and hurt each other's feelings one minute only to flip a switch and hop in bed the next. For most women, we need to make amends verbally and emotionally before any "make-up sex." It can't be flippant or forced, husbands. She needs you to hear what she's saying, and she wants to hear your response, straight from your heart. No nods or "uh-huhs." Tell her what's on your mind and heart. Don't hold back. She wants to connect with you through intimate conversation before physical intimacy. This is counter to how most men work, but it is essential to keeping a thriving and mutually enjoyable sex life in your marriage.

God created sex. He created love. He created life. He created you and He has a beautiful plan for your life and marriage. Regardless of your faith (or lack of faith), I'd encourage you to explore God's plan for sex. Make sexual intimacy and fulfillment a high priority in the marriage and put your spouse's needs ahead of your own needs. Selflessness is the key to a great sex life, and the key to a great friendship and marriage outside the bedroom!

5

NAKED HONESTY

Dave

When Ashley and I were newlyweds, we had just settled comfortably into our little house in Georgetown, Kentucky, next to the college campus where I had graduated a week before our wedding. The "Love Shack," as we called it, was already starting to feel like home, but the age of the house combined with some cracks in the foundation made it possible for critters to find their way inside.

This was a problem for me, because for some weird reason I've always been freaked out by mice. I've even struggled going to Disney World because I'm afraid Mickey is going to start chasing me! It's actually not quite that bad, but it's still a pretty embarrassing fear. At this point in our young marriage, I had done a pretty good job of hiding my fears and frailties from my bride, but she was about to learn in dramatic fashion that her husband wasn't nearly as tough as he pretended to be.

She was doing crunches on the floor in front of the TV while I was doing no physical movement at all lounging in a recliner. Out of the corner of my eye, I saw a quick movement, and I turned my head to see two beady little eyes staring back at me. My fear was staring me in the face.

I gathered my wits and summoned my courage. I was going to take care of this mouse. I refused to be bullied by a rodent in my home in front of my wife. After all, I was the man of the house, and I was about to teach this mouse a lesson. This was a moment of destiny!

I tiptoed to the kitchen and found a large pot and started moving toward the mouse. In hindsight, I'm not entirely sure what I was planning to do with the pot. I think I was planning to capture the mouse under the pot, and then I was hoping Ashley would know what to do from there.

As I took a step toward Mickey, he saw me and made his move. I remember thinking to myself that mice are much faster than you'd think. He started running toward Ashley, who was still on the floor doing sit-ups, but he didn't see her because he was looking back toward me as he ran. Before I could say anything to warn her, the mouse had run onto Ashley's side and scurried his little rodent feet up onto her stomach.

At this point, all chaos broke loose. There was literally shrieking, screaming, and crying. It was a full-blown, hysterical meltdown. Finally, Ashley had to say, "Dave, pull yourself together! It is just a mouse!"

She's still the brave one in the relationship.

We survived the mouse attack and we've laughed about it a lot since then, but that incident also taught me a valuable lesson. If I had been honest with Ashley in the beginning about my fear of mice, the humiliation would have been less severe. When we are vulnerable and transparent with our spouse about everything (even something as small as fear of mice) we set ourselves up for a solid partnership instead of a pattern of secrets.

Unfortunately, many people live a life full of fear and secrecy instead of being led by honesty and love. Secrecy ruins relationships. In fact, it is often the very reason why a relationship ends. Secrecy clouds our judgment and erodes the honesty, trust, and intimacy in our marriage. Honesty, however, heals relationships. It makes us feel secure, sets a positive course for our lives, and chases away our fears in the process.

I believe most (if not all) of us have a fear of being honest, and those fears, if left unchecked, can rob our marriage and our lives of peace and joy. A *naked marriage* requires unfiltered honesty and both spouses giving the *secret-free guarantee* to one another. This means there is never a time or place for secrets in your marriage—unless you are planning a surprise party for your spouse. Secrecy is the enemy of intimacy *and* naked honesty.

Ashley

Sometimes we are afraid because we don't know how to tell our spouse that we are struggling in a certain area. Early in our marriage, I logged into our computer and discovered that Dave had been looking at porn. I couldn't believe what I saw. My heart was beating out of my chest, and I seriously thought that somebody had broken into our home and surfed the web for porn. Not Dave. Not my Dave. We had a great marriage—at least I thought we did.

All I could think was, *How could he do this to me? To us? Am I not enough for him? Am I not pretty/skinny/sexy enough? Doesn't he know this is wrong? Didn't he know this would hurt me?*

I took an hour or so to process what I eventually realized and accepted as the truth: Dave had been looking at porn for a while. He had a porn addiction. My Dave. My husband. My hero.

I knew I had to address it. I called him at work and simply asked if he had something to tell me. He immediately confessed to the porn. It was like he'd been waiting for me to find out. He told me that he was glad it was out in the open now, and that he knew it was wrong. I would love to tell you that the days that followed were easy, but they weren't. I was so hurt. I felt ugly and unwanted. I could tell that Dave felt horrible about it. He'd wanted to stop doing this a long time ago, but he said he just couldn't stop through his own willpower. As a Christian, he understood that he was lusting after the women in those images. He knew what Jesus stated so clearly in the Bible that to lust after a woman is committing adultery in your heart. It goes directly against our marriage vows.

Husbands, I share this with you, not to point fingers or to make you feel bad. I share this because I want you to know what your porn habit does to your wife. It breaks her heart. It makes her feel like you cheated on her. It makes her doubt her beauty and sexual appeal. It causes her to have a deep insecurity with your marriage. It causes her anxiety and even depression. It makes her feel cheap, and she sees you as sleazy. It fractures the trust she has in you, and it immediately makes her lose respect for you.

You may tell yourself the lies that so many other husbands in our culture believe. Lies like:

I'm not hurting anyone.

I'm not actually sleeping with another person, so it's not cheating.

What's wrong with me spicing up my sex life?

This is something I do alone, so it doesn't affect her.

Porn actually enhances my sex life, because it gives me ideas for what we can do in the bedroom.

I'm a grown man, and I can do whatever I want to do. It's none of her business.

It's okay if I look at porn to meet my needs, because she doesn't want to have sex as frequently as I do.

All of these are excuses that mask a *huge* problem and keep husbands intertwined in a terrible habit that can become a full-blown addiction. Husbands, if you are looking at porn, please stop and get help immediately. Go confess this to your wife. Don't hide it anymore. Seek God's forgiveness and your wife's forgiveness.

Then, take the steps necessary to regain her trust. Put accountability in place. Remove computers or other devices from hidden places. Get blockage software that will alarm a trusted friend or your wife any time you look up porn on your computer. Get rid of any television channels that show porn at night. Be willing to do whatever it takes to beat this and save your marriage. You can do this if you are willing to put in the work. You must show your wife that you only have eyes for her. Show her that you want her and love her with all your heart. Give her your time and attention daily.

Those porn stars can't love you back. Don't trade the love of your life for a temporary, empty fix. Go to your wife and talk about your sexual desires and needs. Listen when she shares hers as well. Work together on having a God-honoring and sexually satisfying marriage. Don't settle for a counterfeit image to fulfill a need that only your wife should meet. Porn is never the answer. It doesn't spice things up. It chokes out real intimacy between a husband and wife. Please know that there is hope. Dave and I grew stronger through this struggle, and you can too! If porn is a struggle in your marriage, please get help. Naked honesty takes courage, and I know you can do it. You are not alone.

Dave

I was first exposed to pornography as a teenager, which fits with the statistics, because I've read that as many as 95 percent of all teens will view explicit pornography (either accidentally or on purpose) at least once before they graduate from high school. Whatever the most accurate stats may be, the obvious truth is that it's everywhere and it's having a huge impact on people and specifically on marriages.

Porn is a controversial issue because some people view it as pure evil while others view it as harmless entertainment and even a helpful aid in "spicing up" things in your sex life. The truth is that porn will hurt you and harm your present and future relationships. Some believe that being in a healthy marriage to an attractive spouse will remove the temptation. But porn doesn't train you to be satisfied by a healthy relationship; it warps your mind to never be satisfied. Porn is not harmless fantasy, and it programs your mind to think of sex as an animalistic act with many partners and no emotional attachments. It's an enemy of intimacy.

I know some people may feel like having naked honesty

about porn is hopeless because porn is addictive and you feel like you will never be free of it. The truth is that you can be set free, but you must rely on God's power instead of your own willpower. That's what I had to do.

As a teenager, I would go through a vicious cycle of looking at porn and then feeling guilty and hating myself and staying away by sheer willpower for as long as I could, but then return to it again. This continued through college. Sometimes there were long stints in between my "relapses" which gave me the false sense of security in believing I had overcome it, but I learned repeatedly that I had not overcome it.

Eventually, I bought into the myth that once I got married, it would cure itself, because having a beautiful wife (which I do) would automatically remove the temptation of wanting to look at anyone else. But the secret and shameful cycle continued even after I married the love of my life the week after graduating college. I had shattered her trust and I felt hopelessly ashamed.

As painful as it was to have my secret out in the open, it had to happen to start the healing process. I only wish I'd have had the courage to confess before getting caught. Regardless, getting caught was a gift from God because once the lies are dragged out into the light, even though it hurts at first, it's the first step toward healing. That was more than a decade ago, and thankfully, God and my wife both showed me a lot of grace, which has helped me break free. It took trusting God and putting safeguards and accountabilities in place to retrain my thinking, and today I'm so thankful to be living without that secret shame and constant temptation eating away at me.

If you're reading this and you're currently struggling, you are not alone! The first step is to admit that it's wrong and that you want to make it right. You can overcome this, but don't try to do it alone. Have *naked honesty*. Confess it to your spouse and to God. Ask forgiveness and put safeguards in place right away.

Ashley

Let's face it. We are all visual creatures, and nudity draws us in like flies to a bright light. This isn't inherently a bad thing. In fact, God made human beings this way on purpose. He made us sexual so that we can experience intimate pleasure with our spouse and possibly have children one day. We are supposed to appreciate the naked body. We are wired to desire sex. It isn't gross; it's beautiful. Unfortunately, our culture often represents it as everything but the amazing gift that it is.

Recently, I watched part of an episode of a reality show that follows the glamorous lives of several famous married women. You might know what show I'm referring to, and it can be addicting to watch. During this show, one housewife was discussing what she described as the secret to her seventeen-year marriage. She said that they both "worked at it" and did things to "spice things up" including watching porn together on a regular basis. She then commented that most of her friends didn't watch porn with their spouses, and she thinks that everyone would have better marriages if they watched it together. I honestly couldn't believe how comfortable she was in admitting that this was a regular practice in her marriage. Even if it were true, most people wouldn't admit it on national television. She was not only admitting it, she was celebrating it and even recommending it. I couldn't help but ask myself, *Is porn really becoming this socially acceptable?*

Surprisingly, more women are consuming porn these days. The more I've thought about this, I've realized that this famous housewife's view of porn might be more common than I think. She's willing to call porn what it is in front of millions of people, instead of giving it another name or denying her use of it all together. In Matthew 5:28, Jesus gives us a sober warning against lust when He tells us, "But I tell you that anyone who looks at a woman lustfully has already committed adultery with her in his heart" (NIV). The same goes for women looking at men lustfully.

Many women believe porn is harmless, but it's not. We tell ourselves it is harmless because we aren't engaging in the act, but Jesus clearly raises the standard for Christians here and states that thinking about it is just as sinful as doing it. He doesn't tell us this to be a huge buzzkill or to make life extra hard; He is trying to teach us how to guard our minds and hearts against sexual sin. As Christian wives, we are called to only have eyes and longings for our husbands. Allowing ourselves to be gripped by the lustful thoughts that are sure to come from these seemingly harmless, sexually driven novels or movies only train our minds and hearts to be unsatisfied with our own sex lives. It's so easy to compromise our beliefs when it comes to this. I too have read a little too much, looked a little too long, and pondered longer than I should have. That is exactly what lust does to us. It seems so innocent at the time, but it is an act of subtle disobedience that only leads us down a road of insecurity and emptiness, not to mention broken relationships.

Throughout our marriage ministry, Dave and I have talked to many couples contemplating divorce. When we tried to get to the root of their marital issues, they would often share that they had not had sex for months or even years. In many of these situations, the husband was frequently looking at porn and the wife was filling the void with novels, movies, and nights out with girl friends. They had lost interest in each other, and they considered themselves to be "out of love."

What they didn't see was the common denominator: lust. They had stopped wanting each other, so they were looking to fill their sexual desires elsewhere. Sometimes, these husbands and wives would end up having full-blown emotional or physical affairs, which only made the road to healing much more difficult.

I am not sharing all of this to make anyone feel guilty or hopeless because I know otherwise. God loves us and understands us. He will forgive the repentant. There is hope. I have seen husbands with a hidden porn addiction find the road to healing and restore their marriages. I know wives who have turned away from a lifestyle filled with lust and a loveless marriage only to find that they can have a completely fulfilling marriage on all levels with God's blessing. We don't have to accept whatever our culture considers as socially acceptable. If we want our marriages to be strong, we must turn our hearts and minds to God and He will help us to keep our eyes, minds, and hearts from wandering. He will bless all aspects of our marriages, including the sexual. You don't need porn or some made-up steamy novel to spice up your marriage anyway. So, let's keep movie characters, empty novel fantasies, and ridiculous porn scenarios out of our bedroom and enjoy the beautiful intimate union that we can have with our spouse. True intimacy starts with naked honesty.

Dave

We work with a lot of couples and we know that not all intimacy and honesty issues have to do with porn. Sometimes, naked honesty is sharing with your spouse that you need help in another area. Overcoming any kind of addiction is hard, but naked honesty allows a husband and wife to grow closer through the challenges they face—because they face them together.

Not long ago, I received a mysterious voicemail from a pastor friend of mine. He lives in another city and we rarely hear from each other, so I was a little surprised when his message said he needed to talk to me about something and he didn't want to do it over the phone. We scheduled a meeting and when the day arrived, my friend showed up right on time. It was good to see him, but there was a tension he was wearing on his face instead of his usual laid-back smile. We exchanged some awkward pleasantries and then sat down in my office to talk. I asked him what was going on, and he took a deep breath followed by a long silence as he searched for the words.

What he said next took me completely by surprise. He

gathered his composure and then spoke. I believe it was the first time he had ever said these words out loud and even as he said them, the reality of the situation seemed to shock him just as it was shocking me.

He said, "My wife is a closet alcoholic. I believe she is also addicted to pain pills. It all started out innocently. She'd have a glass of wine or two at night to help her relax before going to bed. On some nights, she'd have a little bit more, but I never really kept track and never thought there was a real problem. During her daily wine habit, she injured her back in a minor car accident and the doctor prescribed her some pain medication. She took what was prescribed, but then I soon noticed she was taking more than the prescribed dosage. She would run through her entire prescription in a week and then do whatever she could to get more pills to last her for the rest of the month. She has managed to get through most days functioning at work and in the community, but some nights I'll find her passed out in a closet. I don't know how much she's drinking or how many pills she's taking, but I know it's a serious problem. She's been lying to me and to others. She's always been the most honest person I know, but I can't trust anything she says anymore. She's hiding things, and I'm terrified I'm going to walk in and find her dead one day. I feel powerless. I'm not sure when or how it all spiraled out of control. I feel so guilty for not taking more action sooner. She's always been so strong, and I just figured she would pull through this. I also wanted to protect her reputation at church and in the community and for her job, but now this is a full-blown crisis and I have no idea what to do."

Substance abuse and addiction has touched nearly everyone. Most of us have had a loved one who has battled addiction, and some of us have battled it ourselves or have a spouse who has struggled. When addiction appears in your marriage, it's vital to take immediate action and to have naked honesty with your spouse. Like my pastor friend, if your spouse is caught in substance abuse or addiction, please take action.

Each situation is unique, but the first step in most marriage issues is naked *honesty*. Talk about what's going on. Tell your spouse their behavior is getting out of control and if they won't get help on their own, out of love for them, you'll have to intervene and get others involved. Make a plan together and if they won't listen or won't stick to it, take further action to intervene.

My friend was wise to reach out to me. It was a burden no one should carry alone, and I'm so glad he reached out. If your spouse is caught up in addiction, reach out to some trusted friends and relatives. Don't put it all over social media. Protect your spouse's reputation, but even more important, protect your spouse by getting help. That help will require enlisting the help of others who love you and love your spouse.

While the help of a few loved ones is important, you may also need medical or psychological help. My friend was able to connect to an addiction support group through our church and a rehabilitation program where his wife was able to get clean and sober over a period of six weeks. She needed the intervention of some trusted loved ones to help her see the crisis of her situation and to help her finally admit she was powerless to overcome her addiction alone. Addiction is a monster that can't be battled alone. There's strength in community through groups like AA, family support, and church groups such as Celebrate Recovery. For both spouses, these groups along with the love of friends and family can make all the difference.

Nearly all addiction recovery programs point people to a higher power. In case you haven't met Him, the higher power's name is Jesus and He is with you in the storm. Pray, read God's Word, and trust that the Lord will carry you and your spouse through any difficulty in marriage. Naked honesty transforms marriage. So, trust God will carry you and your spouse and get honest!

Ashley

Naked honesty about any form of addiction is the only way to start the healing process. But there is one area of secrecy in marriage that is the most gut-wrenching and detrimental—*affairs*. Infidelity doesn't "just happen" one day in a bedroom; it begins in the mind.

It starts innocently. The two of you just connect. You have a lot in common and before you know it, you start looking forward to more encounters with your "friend." And that's all he or she is in your eyes—at least, for now. That's what you tell yourself in your heart of hearts. You don't want to hurt your spouse, but this "friend" is such a good listener and makes you feel loved, desired, respected—wanted. Things you haven't felt with your spouse in a long time, but you've never really talked about it.

You start spending more and more time with this person and even go to lunch a few times. You tell yourself it's okay because, after all, you are just friends, right? But you find yourself sharing more personal stories than you intend to and locking eyes longer than you should. During your encounters, time tends to stand still, and every day you find yourself thinking about this person more and more.

Before you know it, you realize that some major boundaries have been crossed, and you are afraid to have naked honesty with your spouse.

Does any of this sound familiar? If so, please know that you are not alone.

There's nothing wrong with finding a kindred spirit in another person, but it's a slippery, nosedive of a slope when this close friendship is with someone of the opposite sex who is not your spouse. This may sound harsh and even ridiculous to you. I mean, we're all adults, right? We should be able to control ourselves and be "friends" with whoever we want—right?

Well, not exactly.

Would you be okay with your spouse having this same kind

of *friendship*? Same conversations? Same encounters? Same attraction?

Probably not, right?

I know you love your spouse and would never hurt him/her on purpose. But please hear me. Being close friends with someone of the opposite sex isn't good for your marriage at all. As one who works with struggling married couples on a daily basis, it breaks my heart to see these "friendships" wounding marriages time and time again.

Close friendships with those of the opposite sex open your heart and marriage to a world of hurt, because your frequent conversations with this friend are like cords of a rope—each one making the connection stronger and more intimate. Your longing for more interactions is evidence of your desire to know this person more—this is dangerous territory. Again, affairs don't start in the bedroom, they always start in the mind! If you allow your mind to play out fantasies, you're giving a piece of your heart to the object of that fantasy and you're opening the door for the fantasy to become a reality.

If you allow this secrecy to continue then, honestly, it is only natural for this connection to continue to progress to a physical, sexual relationship over time, unless you are intentional about putting boundaries in place and creating distance between you and your friend. The excitement and allure of this new friendship is intoxicating and is harder to let go the longer it carries on.

I don't tell you all of this to make you feel bad. I tell you these truths to warn you and keep you from doing something that could devastate your marriage. If you have a "friend" like this, then please be honest with your spouse about what is going on and do whatever it takes to put some distance between you and that "friend." Create healthy boundaries and fight for your marriage. Honestly connect with your spouse— not this *friend*.

If that's you, if you recognize that you are in pretty deep

with this friend of the opposite sex and possibly have romantic feelings for him/her, then you need to confess this romantic affair to your spouse and seek Christian marriage counseling immediately. This may be very difficult, and it will be hard for your spouse to process. But it's better to confess this now then to engage in a full-blown sexual affair later. The two of you can get through this when you decide to get honest and do what is necessary to rebuild trust. Don't let this opposite-sex friend distract you from your commitment to your spouse. Your marriage is worth fighting for. Let this be a wakeup call. It's not too late! Secrecy is the enemy of intimacy in marriage. Confess to your spouse anything you've been hiding and start working hard to rebuild trust.

Dave

Secrets truly are the enemy of intimacy. A good friend of mine recently confided in me that he cheated on his wife a few years ago. He's been carrying guilt and shame over the affair every day since the one-night stand with a coworker, but he said that he's decided not to confess this to his wife because it would only hurt her. In his mind, he has justified his secrecy as a way to protect his wife and his marriage.

We have worked with married couples from all over the world, and we've found that my friend's decision to keep big secrets from his spouse is a common mindset. We live in a time where people value personal privacy over total transparency in marriage, and this secretive mindset is having some massive repercussions in the long-term health of our relationships.

Ashley and I know that naked honesty is always best, and for my friend, confessing the whole truth to his wife is far better than living with this secret. Friends, have the courage to pursue greater transparency and trust in your own marriage. If you made a bad choice in the past, please don't cover it up by making a bad choice every single day to hide it deliberately and dishonestly. No matter what it might cost you, the truth is always worth telling.

Naked honesty in marriage means having nothing to hide from each other. It means full transparency. It means giving your spouse an all-access key to your heart, your mind, your hopes, your fears, and every other part of your life. If you want to experience love and intimacy without limits, get naked (which also means getting honest). Secrets create invisible landmines in your marriage that will explode in unintended ways.

When we carry around secrets of any kind, those secrets will not stay buried. They leave a residue on our attitudes and behaviors; they tend to expose themselves in unlikely ways. Most of our secrets will come out eventually and then we have to deal with the aftermath of the secret itself plus the additional breach of trust that came with each day we chose to keep hiding it. But confession shows courage and character. Secrets show deception and dishonesty. We want to hide our mistakes, sins, and flaws from our spouse (and everyone else), but when we try to keep something hidden, it numbs our own conscience in the process. Secrets don't make us stronger; they make us weaker (and they weaken our marriages as well).

In marriage, any form of secrecy is really an act of infidelity. In marriage, secrets are just as dangerous as outright lies. Every day you choose to keep something hidden from your spouse, you're essentially committing a form of infidelity (*infidelity* really just means *broken trust*). When we value our own privacy at the expense of the sacred vows we made to our spouse, we're chipping away at the foundation of trust that every strong marriage must be built upon. The moment you send a text message or visit a website you hope your spouse doesn't find out about, you're already in dangerous territory. But a painful truth is always better than a hidden lie.

It hurts to confess a painful secret and it hurts to hear one, but it is far worse to carry the weight of a secret sin. Whenever we let something live in the dark, it controls us, but once we bring it out into the light, it can't control us any longer. Have the courage to confess. Your marriage will get stronger when you both stop hiding things from each other.

When we keep secrets to protect the marriage, we're actually weakening the marriage. We're building the relationship on a faulty foundation. If you really want to have naked honesty in your marriage, then take the *secret-free guarantee*. Stop hiding things. Bring it all out into the open. It might be a painful process, but it could take your relationship to a new level of health, wholeness, and happiness.

6

NAKED SCARS

Dave

When I was in the eighth grade, I had a crush on a girl in my class named Angie. I was a pretty dorky kid in middle school, but despite my adolescent awkwardness, I managed to summon the courage to start a conversation with her whenever I could. My so-called courage was actually just a combination of raging hormones and unrealistic optimism, but it felt like courage in my eighth-grade brain, and that was good enough for me.

My voice would crack, and my palms would get sweaty, but with each conversation she would politely smile while she dodged the tiny spit particles flying off my braces as I spoke. I interpreted her smile to mean that she wanted to spend the rest of her life with me. We had never actually had a conversation that lasted more than thirty-seconds, but I was pretty sure she was my soul mate. I was convinced that when she looked at me, she didn't see my braces and acne; she saw Prince Charming.

Our love story was off to a stellar start until the fateful day when everything unraveled in one of the most terrifying moments of my life. We were standing in science class, where I had cornered her for a chat, when I suddenly felt a draft of air on my legs. I heard laughter behind me, and Angie's face turned a bright shade of red. She covered her face and giggled and quickly ran off, leaving me standing there trying to figure out what had just happened. I looked down slowly, and to my horror, my sweatpants were down at my ankles.

Yes, I wore sweatpants to school, don't judge me! They were comfortable, and in the early nineties in central Kentucky, they were still a socially acceptable wardrobe option for middle school. That was, however, the last day I ever wore sweatpants anywhere. You just can't trust the drawstring on those things.

This particular wardrobe malfunction, though, was not the result of a faulty drawstring; this was an act of sabotage. My "friend" Nick had grabbed my pants from behind and yanked them to the floor. God had mercy on me that day and somehow kept my Fruit of the Loom underwear from making the trip along with my pants. Had my tighty-whiteys gone to the floor too, I'd probably still be in counseling over the whole ordeal.

I pulled my pants back up to my waist with ninja-like reflexes, but the damage had been done. Humiliation had been inflicted. I had been in the most vulnerable and exposed position possible, and instead of receiving compassion and encouragement from this girl I really liked, I felt the sting of rejection. We never really talked after that, but it was probably more because of my own embarrassment than anything else.

I share this funny story not because it's an example of a true scar, but because it paints the picture of vulnerability in our lives and how our view of ourselves can be shaped by our past experiences. Marriage requires vulnerability, and when we feel like we've been in an exposed position and then experienced pain, shame, or rejection, our defense mechanisms can actually work against us—sabotaging our marriages.

We tend to militantly safeguard certain parts of ourselves to prevent the same kind of humiliation or hurt we have felt in the past. I know I wore a belt very tightly for years after that sweatpants incident.

We've all faced many relational challenges far more significant than an embarrassing middle-school prank. When we've been rejected, hurt, abandoned, or abused by the very people who should have been protecting us, the ramifications can be deep and long lasting. If you've experienced the sting of a relational wound, you know exactly the kind of pain I'm talking about.

Ashley

The more you love someone, the greater access they have to your heart, and therefore, they have a greater ability to potentially hurt you. This can be scary! However, until you give a person the ability to hurt you by being vulnerable with them, you'll never be able to truly experience a beautifully intimate and committed relationship with that person. This reality keeps some people from wholeheartedly committing to and embracing marriage, because they're trying to protect their heart from being wounded again. If we're not careful, our wounds from the past will create new wounds in our marriage—perpetuating pain and distance in our relationship—until we become intentional about healing from the past and moving forward in a healthy way. As Dave and I have interacted with people who have experienced childhood abuse, marital infidelity, or any form of pain and disappointment from the past, we've noticed that many have developed a defense mechanism we call "emotional sunburn."

Have you ever gone to the beach and forgotten to apply sunscreen? We used to live in Florida, and this would happen to Dave all the time. He'd think it wasn't a big deal because he'd only be exposed to the sun for a short time, but hours later, his unprotected skin would be lobster red. He would quickly put on a T-shirt to cover up, but without fail, someone in the family would come give him a slap on the back or a hug that was a little too rough and he'd scream in pain.

It felt like he was screaming at us in anger, but he wasn't. It wasn't about us at all. He was sunburned and hurting. We just happened to touch him where he was already hurting, and he needed time to heal.

So many of us have this emotional sunburn—this invisible

burn all over our hearts and souls, maybe because of things that have happened to us or because of things that we have done. And our spouse, due to their near proximity to us, will sometimes touch us where we are already wounded, and we'll get angry. Therefore, we need to create an environment in our marriage where there is a lot of love and patience. Instead of picking at our spouse's burns, we need to be rubbing aloe on their scars—creating a safe place for them to heal. We need to pray for them and ask God to heal their hearts. He is the ultimate healer.

Sadly, many of us have emotional sunburn all over our heart from being burned in our past. These past scars or wounds, if left untreated, can cause us to overreact in unhealthy ways to our loved ones, pushing others away to protect ourselves. Whatever you may have done or whatever may have been done to wound you in the past, healing is possible. God wants you to experience vulnerability and love with your spouse. He wants you to experience a rich, meaningful marriage. He wants to bring you to a place of healing, so you can experience a loving marriage in its fullness.

Dave

What if you are in a marriage where your *spouse* is the one causing the wound or scars? I received a message on Facebook the other day from a man who is suffering in secret. He is part of a large but invisible fraternity of which he never wanted to be a member. He's among the countless men who feel bullied or abused by their wives.

Ashley and I talk openly about abuse in marriage, but the abuse we typically focus on is the physical or emotional abuse husbands can inflict on wives. Most of the culture's conversation around abuse follows this same narrative. Certainly, there are statistical and practical reasons to talk more about marital abuse against women, but we must also recognize that many men are suffering too.

When a man feels bullied or abused in marriage, he often feels complex emotions, which include pain inflicted by his wife's behavior plus shame and isolation, because he feels like his very manhood has been stolen from him. For a man to confess to anyone that he's being bullied or abused in marriage requires an enormous amount of vulnerability. There's a stigma attached to abused men that can carry the unfair assumption, *If you were a "real man" then nobody would be able to abuse you or mistreat you. There must be something wrong with you.*

All abuse victims (male and female) carry many complex emotions and scars. Victim shaming certainly occurs with both genders and it needs to stop altogether. We must develop more compassion so victims of any form of abuse or bullying in marriage will have the courage to step out of the shadows and share their stories. Every situation is unique and there's a broad spectrum of controlling and/or abusive behaviors, so it's difficult to prescribe a one-size-fits-all menu of options.

The need to control usually stems from deeper issues. If you are a husband married to a wife who is bullying or obsessively controlling, the most helpful resource I could suggest as a first step is a book called *Boundaries* by Dr. John Townsend and Dr. Henry Cloud. You need to establish some loving but firm boundaries with your wife to let her know that her behavior is undermining the sacred partnership of the marriage and if it continues unchanged, the marriage itself is in danger of unraveling. Know that in some cases, a wife who has a need to control or bully is herself dealing with emotional scars and/or physical health issues. Seeking counseling and medical help to rule out any underlying psychological, hormonal, or physical issues might help solve some of the negative behavior. There are times when a wife is caught up in the habit of control and she's blind to it. She doesn't even know she's doing it.

When any form of physical abuse is happening in marriage, a massive line has been crossed and immediate action needs to be taken to ensure safety. In admitting the abuse, a man isn't becoming less of a man. He's being more of a man by getting the help he needs and getting his wife the help she needs. Physical abuse is a sign that a marriage is out of control and can only be saved with intervention.

When a wife's words are a stream of negativity and criticism, it can make a man feel like his very soul is being crushed. In some ways, verbal abuse hurts more and leaves deeper scars than physical abuse. If your wife is spewing venom with her words, then along with the book *Boundaries*, counseling is a good choice. One piece of advice you may have never considered is to secretly record your wife and get audio and video evidence of her abusive words. Once you have the evidence, show it to her. Don't start a fight with it; simply say, "It hurts me the way you talk to me. I want to give you the benefit of the doubt in believing you don't realize how you're communicating to me, but here's the hard truth. If you're not willing to make changes or get counseling, I'm going to show this video to some of our loved ones and see if their intervention can convince you to get help. Either way, we're not going to keep living like this."

Often abuse is just a manifestation of addiction. Once drugs, alcohol, or other substances have hijacked a person's mind, that person has lost control. If your wife is addicted, get her the help she needs. By any means, whether it takes an intervention or driving her against her will to a place where she can get help—take drastic action. The bottom line, if there's abuse or bullying of any kind happening in your marriage, don't lose hope. Don't settle for the status quo. Get the help you need.

Ashley

When one spouse is controlling or dominating the vulnerability in the marriage shuts down. And the mistreated spouse feels emotionally wounded, and as they try to heal, there are often some emotional scars left behind. God designed marriage to be a safe place for our heart—not a volatile place.

When we marry our spouse, we enter into a beautiful union where we can no longer think only of ourselves. We must work together to make collective decisions that are best for *both* spouses. One way we can consistently do this effectively is by openly communicating on most decisions. However, I want to point out that this practice requires a delicate balance. Permission is not a word that adults like to use or hear—unless directed toward their children. We ask for permission every day of our lives. In our jobs and in normal life we ask and give permission all day long. It is simply part of life. So, why do some have such an issue with it in their marriage?

If you were to look at some synonyms for *permission* you would read words like *authorization, consent, authority, agreement, approval, blessing, clearance, allowance, tolerance,* or *empowerment.* When I read through these words, they all appear to have favorable meanings by themselves, yet still the term *permission* seems negative to many of us. Why is that? I believe it's because many people have used the act of giving permission in a selfish, unhealthy, or abusive way. If this is the truth, it is no wonder that someone would hate asking for permission—especially from their spouse. Even still, I believe it is a good thing when it is done in a healthy, loving, respectful way. So, how can asking for your spouse's permission go wrong? It goes wrong when the need for *control* is at the heart of it. This is when wounds happen.

Our marriage is a lifelong commitment, not a lifelong sentence. It is a choice. We choose to give and receive love to and from our spouse every day. We shouldn't treat our spouse like some kind of prisoner. We don't make demands; that is not an act of love in marriage, and it certainly doesn't foster a loving environment. We both seek the permission of the other out of love and respect for each other, but this is not to be confused with codependence.

One type of codependent relationship is described as a type of dysfunctional helping relationship where one person supports or enables another person's addiction, poor mental health, immaturity, irresponsibility, or under-achievement. In other words, the person calling the shots within the codependent relationship holds the other partner down by taking advantage of his/her dependency on the alpha in the pairing. This is not healthy and is abusive—resulting in scars. We must never manipulate our spouse by making him/her feel inadequate without our approval or guidance. Again, the asking of permission must be a mutual practice in marriage to cultivate and keep a healthy relationship.

Recently, I received a message from a wife who feels suffocated and disrespected by her husband's need to control her. He tells her what to cook, how to clean, how to discipline the kids, and even what to wear to work. Instead of asking her opinion on things and making decisions as a couple, her husband believes his word is the final one and his wife's thoughts don't need to be part of the equation. Whenever she tries to intervene or exerts her opinion, her husband becomes very angry. They usually end up having a big argument, so she backs down to "keep the peace," and the cycle continues. This husband's controlling approach is scarring his wife's heart and deeply wounding his marriage. This poor wife feels emotionally abused by her husband's demands, and she fears the reaction that she might receive if she questions his decisions. Friends, this is not healthy at all. Marriage is about serving one another in love, and a spouse's desperate need for control goes directly against this.

Control breeds fear, and the Bible is clear that,

There is no fear in love, but perfect love drives out fear.
1 John 4:18 (NIV)

Even so, I have heard some Christian husbands use Bible verses about marital submission to support their need to control, but these husbands are often not remembering or understanding the meaning of the entire passage. In Ephesians 5:21–33, Paul writes:

Submit to one another out of reverence for Christ. Wives, submit yourselves to your own husbands as you do to the Lord. For the husband is the head of the wife as Christ is the head of the church, his body, of which he is the Savior. Now as the church submits to Christ, so also wives should submit to their husbands in everything. Husbands, love your wives, just as Christ loved the church and gave himself up for her to make her holy, cleansing her by the washing with water through the word, and to present her to himself as a radiant church, without stain or wrinkle or any other blemish, but holy and blameless. In this same way, husbands ought to love their wives as their own bodies. He who loves his wife loves himself. After all, no one ever hated their own body, but they feed and care for their body, just as Christ does the church—for we are members of his body. "For this reason a man will leave his father and mother and be united to his wife, and the two will become one flesh." This is a profound mystery—but I am talking about Christ and the church. However, each one of you also must love his wife as he loves himself, and the wife must respect her husband.
(NIV)

It's interesting that Paul first encourages married couples to "submit to one another out of reverence for Christ" before he goes into the specifics of submission (love and respect) for both husbands and wives. And when we read further into these verses, husbands are called to be willing to lay down their lives for their wives, just as Jesus willingly laid down His life for us. Wow! That is a high standard! It even goes on to say that husbands should care for their wives as they care for their own bodies and as Christ cares for the church.

I find this very interesting in light of a husband wanting control in his marriage. You see, controlling someone is not the same thing as caring for someone, especially in marriage. In fact, when a husband strives to control his wife, he is casting her cares, insight, and opinions aside and treating her like a child, or one who doesn't have the maturity or life experience to help make important decisions. Instead of controlling, God has called a husband to love his wife in such a way that he would give his life to protect her physically, emotionally, and spiritually, and this requires servant-hearted tenderness, trust, and respect.

Dave has wisely said that a husband and wife are like two wings on the same bird, with Christ as the head. This is a beautiful image of a husband and wife soaring together, but this will not work unless there are *two* wings. I've never seen a bird fly when one wing is trying to dominate the other wing and hold it down. That bird will never get off the ground. So, what can a wife do when she feels like her husband is always trying to control her?

Well, it starts with having a heart-to-heart, gut-level, honest conversation. The truth is, we are only going to be treated with the level of respect that we have for ourselves, so we cannot keep on making excuses for our spouse's unhealthy behavior toward us. When we don't stand up for ourselves, we only perpetuate the problem. However, we must resist the urge to stand our ground by lashing out and creating an even bigger fight. Instead, calmly tell your husband that his constant need for control hurts your heart and makes you feel unvalued and unloved. If he gets upset and you both can't seem to have a respectful conversation around this issue, it might be time to see a Christian counselor.

It often helps to have a neutral third party walk a husband and wife through a healthy conversation. They can help get to the heart of the issue about why one spouse feels the need to control. Your husband may not even be aware that he's being controlling at all or that his need for control is unhealthy. A Christian counselor can help him to see this, and he/she could help both of you to develop a healthier way to communicate where you both feel heard and understood. In the *naked* marriage, a husband and wife live as one—unified in their commitment, purpose, and vision. We live this out by supporting each other, not by holding down or controlling one another. When both the husband and wife choose to lift one another up, they will soar together, and the scars will begin to heal.

Dave

Scars heal when a husband and wife join in prayer and vulnerability. That is what the naked marriage is all about. Ashley and I are blessed to get to minister to marriages all around the world. We encourage husbands and wives to have full transparency with each other. And we love hearing stories of good news when a couple gets engaged or overcomes a hardship in their marriage, but we also hear many stories of heartbreak from couples facing tragedies like discovering evidence of an affair. Some of the greatest scars a marriage can carry are those left in the aftermath of infidelity.

One day, I opened my inbox and another familiar message came through. It was from a husband who just found out his wife had been having an affair with his best friend. I can't imagine how much this double dose of betrayal must sting. Despite his obvious pain and heartbreak, he was asking about what he could do to try and save the marriage. I told him that I'd be praying for a miracle and then I shared some practical steps to recover and heal from infidelity.

When your spouse has had an emotional or physical affair, the first thing you must do to start the healing process is choose to forgive. This doesn't mean you trust your spouse at this point. Forgiveness and trust are two different things. Forgiveness is simply saying, "Because I love you, I'm choosing to pursue restoration instead of revenge. I'm choosing to pursue healing instead of hatred." Once you have taken this first step, then insist on your spouse breaking off all contact with the other person involved. If your spouse won't break off all contact, there's no opportunity for trust or healing to happen.

For trust to happen, you both need to create a policy of

total transparency in the marriage. This should include account-ability software (like X3Watch or Covenant Eyes) on all phones and devices to block porn and to monitor contacts. Again, your marriage must have the *secret-free guarantee* from both spouses for the marriage to heal. All marriages need complete transparency regardless of whether there's been an affair.

Another vital next step is to go to counseling right away with a professional Christian marriage counselor to help navigate the path to rebuilding trust and intimacy. We also highly encourage couples recovering from an affair to attend a retreat specifically for married couples in crisis. There are many offered throughout the country.

In addition to counseling, prioritize time together to rekin-dle the intimacy in your relationship. Give yourselves lots of time to talk. Pray together. Laugh and cry together. Spend plenty of time alone with your spouse, but don't try to do life alone. You both need a community of support around you, which should include a healthy church home and other trusted people praying for you, giving accountability and support.

Decide in advance that you're not going to give up when it gets hard. There are going to be moments of great pain and emotion even after you think you've "gotten over it." There will be lasting scars and wounds from this kind of betrayal, but you must decide in advance not to keep holding this over your spouse's head. If you're both committed to healing, you will get through this and God's grace will prove to be enough for you both. The peace that Christ brings is more powerful than our worst sins.

As an important addition here, if you're doing everything in your power to forgive your spouse and save your marriage, but your spouse chooses to walk away, please understand that it's not your fault. Do everything you can to promote healing and hope, but if he/she chooses to leave, let them go in peace. They may choose to end the marriage, but that's not the end of *your* story. God has a beautiful plan for you and He will carry you through this.

For those couples where both spouses are willing to move forward together, don't quit! The road will be long, and it will be difficult, but it will be worth the effort! The Lord will give you grace and strength for the journey and this deep scar will become a powerful part of your testimony someday.

Ashley

Some of you have scars on your hearts because of some deeply hurtful words your spouse has said to you. You are finding it hard to heal especially when it feels like almost every conversation with your spouse ends in an argument. When your marriage is struggling, and you are hurting, it can be difficult to talk to your spouse. I hear struggling couples say things like "All we do is fight" or "He just doesn't listen to me" or "She just shouldn't feel that way." These kinds of statements don't get us anywhere. In those times when we can't muster up anything nice or productive to say to one another, we need to switch our go-to communication style.

If you can relate to this, try writing down your feelings on paper first. Read through your letter and rewrite it in the most loving way possible. Have your spouse do the same thing. Then, at a certain point in the day, hand the letter to your spouse and ask him/her to read it. Take his/her letter and read it too. Next, take time and write a response to the letter. Read it, rewrite it, and hand it to him/her. Do this exercise until you both feel like you can have a civil conversation. Then sit down and talk to one another without distractions. Apologize for the hurtful conversations of the past and share your hearts with one another. Do your best to get it all out, and don't interrupt each other. Listen until your spouse is finished with what he/she has to say. Respond in the most loving way possible. When you both take the time to really hear each other out—without interruptions, excuses, accusations, and hurtful words—you will find that it is much easier for you both to get on the same page and moving in the same direction. This will help you to navigate difficult conversations with your spouse as you both pursue healing and honesty in your marriage.

Letting Go

There's a show that Dave and I watch sometimes called *Hoarders*. It's about people who accumulate junk and never get rid of it. Their homes are filled with piles of trash so high that the only things that can navigate around are roaches and rats. The show is both sad and disgusting. On a spiritual level, I think a lot of us live our lives as hoarders.

We don't mean to become hoarders; it just naturally happens over time until one day we're buried under a pile of junk. But we've got to be willing to clear away negative things that are taking up space to make room for new things that will bring peace back into our lives and marriages. Once we make these choices, we'll be able to help others find healing as well.

We need to pray for God to remove the junk, to remove the clutter, and to heal our scars. Once the scars start to heal, it's time to bring in new things to replace them. Colossians 3:12 reads,

> *"Since God chose you to be the holy people he loves, you must clothe yourselves with tenderhearted mercy, kindness, humility, gentleness, and patience."*
> *(NLT)*

We need to ask God to fill our lives with these attributes and be diligent in our efforts to hold onto them for the sake of our marriages. Allow God's Word to renew your mind and give you a new way of thinking that leads to a new way of living and interacting with your spouse. God wants to bring you healing. Trust Him enough to let go of those wounds and scars that are holding you back—those toxic forces sabotaging your marriage. Keep in mind that this isn't a one-time process. The negative clutter and scars have a tendency to keep working their way into our lives, so this should become a lifestyle pattern of clearing out the old (negative stuff) and making room for the new (positive stuff). Don't let your marriage get buried by scars. Let the love of God and the love of your spouse sweep through your life and replace that junk with joy and hope.

We've all experienced scars. Perhaps you have lived in perpetual pain inflicted over a lifetime of abuse and betrayal by those you loved most, or perhaps you've been fortunate to have relatively few moments of heartbreak. Either way, none of us are immune to pain from the past, and all of us can benefit from healing. The health of your present and future relationships may hinge on how you choose to address the issue of healing from your past.

Healing looks different at different stages in the process, but I want to address those who are in a current crisis and need some critical care. When we're scarred, isolated, or angry, we tend to make our worst decisions; so, in the midst of the storm you're in right now, please let me give you some perspective. The decisions you'll make in the days to come might set the course for the next chapter of your life. In those moments of heartbreak, you'll find yourself standing at a critical crossroads.

One choice will lead you down a path of bitterness. You'll be tempted to push loved ones away. You might even be tempted to push God away because you blame Him for the pain you are experiencing. The path of bitterness might feel liberating at first, but it will prove to be a trap in the end.

The other path is a road to healing. It's a road where you choose to trust God even when you don't understand what's happening. It's a road where you'll be willing to use your own pain as a way to help others find healing, which will ultimately help you find healing too—*choose the path of healing*. And yes, we need to have vulnerability with our spouse to move forward in the path of healing, but ultimately healing from scars isn't the result of mere time and effort. It comes when we put our trust in the healer of our hearts—Jesus.

Jesus was the physical embodiment of love and healing. He wants to heal our hearts—every scar, every heartbreak. Jesus heals, and He wants to heal your marriage. An encounter with Jesus always has the power to bring healing. When love is present, healing is present. It won't always look miraculous, but it will always make a difference. Friends, surrender your scars to Jesus and allow Him to heal your naked scars today.

7

NAKED AND ALONE

Dave

Of all human relationships, God designed marriage to be the most powerful and intimate expression of unity and love. Genesis 2:18 reads,

> *"Then the Lord God said, 'It is not good for the man to be alone. I will make a helper who is just right for him."*
> *(NLT)*

Marriage mirrors the type of relationship God wants to have with us and that is one of partnership, friendship, and unity. We weren't created to be alone, and after God created Eve and she was joined to Adam, God said, "It is good." A unified marriage is a strong marriage.

The best way I can describe unity in marriage is through what I call the *loveseat* principle. Now, to give you an idea of what this looks like, I want you to visualize a loveseat and then two individual chairs off to the side of the loveseat, just like in most living rooms. These pieces of furniture represent a few different "postures," or relational dynamics, that a marriage can have.

The first posture is a husband and wife who choose to approach life from the loveseat. Imagine them sitting side by side. They are unified. They're serving each other, communicating openly and honestly, and completely connected. When problems arise, they choose to face them together and work through it.

The second posture is a husband and wife who choose to approach life from the individual chairs, or *single* seats. Imagine the space between these chairs. Now, picture them on wheels—drifting further and further apart. Those in the single seats are focused on their own needs and prone to blaming each other for the marriage not being what they think it should be. When hard times come, they tell themselves that they should just call it quits because they are better off by themselves anyway.

The third posture is the loneliest one. This occurs when one spouse chooses to approach life from the loveseat while the other spouse chooses to be in the single seat. The spouse in the loveseat wants the marriage to work. They are praying and doing all they know how to do to fight for their marriage. But, sadly, they are the only one fighting for it. The spouse in the single seat has stopped making their marriage a priority. They don't want to work through it because of their pride and preferences.

This is a frustrating and hurtful dynamic to be in, but the good news is that with God there is always hope. He can help those in the single seats to stand up and join each other in the loveseat. He softens hardened hearts and brings dead things—even lifeless, out of sync marriages—back to life!

Ashley and I believe that every marriage is in one of these three postures, and it is our hope and prayer that all married couples come back together to that loveseat and cultivate a unified marriage.

We want couples to come to the place where they can say, "It's not all about me and my own needs. I want to serve you, even when I don't feel like it and even when these gestures of goodwill aren't necessarily reciprocated. I want to serve you and give you my best even when you are not in a position to give back. I don't want to treat you the way you may be treating me. I want to treat you the way God treats me. God gives me His best, even when I'm at my worst. And I want to strive to do the same for you."

Friends, God calls us to love each other the way He loves us. And the happiest marriages have a husband and a wife who both understand this principle and do their best to live it out. One way we can live out this principle is by starting each day with asking our spouse, "How can I help you today?"

When both the husband and wife make it their mission to serve one another, their hearts are going to be filled up in the process and their marriage will thrive. When a couple takes on this mindset, which goes against our selfish nature, real and lasting transformation happens. And the marriage will be happier and healthier.

Now, just because you are in the loveseat doesn't mean that you aren't going to have disagreements, but when you are in that loveseat you are going to handle those disagreements in a healthier way and talk through them until you both reach a resolution. But if both of you are separated in those single seats which we also refer to as the *me* seats, you are only thinking about your own feelings and your own "rights."

When you and your spouse aren't unified, you won't handle the disagreements well. Unity doesn't mean uniformity. A husband and wife certainly won't always see eye to eye. But when you both choose to approach life from the loveseat, you consciously choose to face your struggles together—to talk, to listen, to monitor and adjust, and to get help when necessary—and you remain unified and connected.

It's important that we think about and identify where we are in our marriages. Be honest. Ask yourself if you are in the *loveseat* with your spouse or if you are in the *me* seat thinking about your own needs and agenda. In marriage there is no *his* problem or *her* problem. It is always *our problem*. We aren't meant to be in the *me* seats and feeling *alone* in our marriages. A husband and wife should be unified in the *loveseat*—loving, respecting, and serving one another.

Jesus is the greatest example of how we are supposed to

love, respect, and serve each other. Jesus is the embodiment of love and He showed us that love is much more about action and commitment than it is about feelings. This is important as it relates to the loveseat. We must commit to be unified with one another no matter how we are feeling. Jesus pursued us passionately and then displayed the ultimate love by dying in our place on the cross. And the Bible specifically calls husbands to love their wives with that same type of selfless love. Ephesians 5:25 reads,

> *"For husbands, this means love your wives, just as Christ loved the church. He gave up his life for her."*
> *(NLT)*

Jesus was a king, but He laid down His rights to be served and instead served others. As husbands, we are called to serve our wives. In practical terms, this means placing her needs ahead of our wants and needs. It means prioritizing her ahead of our hobbies or even our careers. It means being willing to do dishes, fold laundry, or whatever else is needed to support her.

> *But among you it will be different. Whoever wants to be a leader among you must be your servant, and whoever wants to be first among you must become your slave. For even the Son of Man came not to be served but to serve others and to give his life as a ransom for many.*
> *Matthew 20:26–28 (NLT)*

Jesus was described as a shepherd. In His culture, a shepherd was one who would protect the sheep from any form of attack, even if it meant risking his own life in the process. This type of love in action doesn't happen from the *me* seat. It only happens in the *loveseat*. As husbands, we are called to be the protectors of our wives, and we can't effectively do this unless we are "all in" and fully committed to the marriage and unified with her in the loveseat.

While God gave you those manly muscles for a reason,

physical protection is only one part of the equation. Husbands need to be emotional and spiritual protectors as well. This means speaking words of encouragement and hope instead of belittlement or demand. It also means accepting God's call to lead your wife into deeper spiritual maturity. Jesus provides every need both great and small. He set the example of the husband as provider by giving sight to a blind man, giving food to the hungry masses that hadn't eaten lunch, and even giving His own life to bring salvation.

Providing financially is one part of this, but don't use that as an excuse to work so much that you are absent from your marriage. The greatest gift Jesus provided was Himself, and the greatest gift you can provide your wife is *yourself*. Part of providing means simply providing your own presence. Your wife can do with less of almost anything if it means having more of you. Jesus is the standard-bearer for life and relationships for both husbands and wives. His example of selfless service, honesty, and love is exactly what we need to be in the loveseat with our spouse.

Ashley

Wives, some of you might be reading this and thinking, "My husband is just not emotionally available! He won't join me on the loveseat." These are words that so many wives have said about their husbands, only to be left feeling misunderstood and unloved. Most husbands don't fully understand what their wives mean by "emotionally available," and it kind of freaks them out.

Instead of striving to be more emotionally available, many men sidestep the issue and try to avoid it altogether by throwing themselves into work and hobbies. But this only makes the problem worse, and it often leads to a wife being emotionally neglected. Then the wife pulls away sexually because she doesn't feel an emotional connection to her husband, and a negative cycle of misunderstanding, hurt, and neglect is formed.

Wives, does this sound familiar? If so, you are not alone, and the good news is there are steps you can take to help your husband emotionally connect with you. First of all, it's important that you take the right approach when you inform your husband that you don't feel like the two of you are emotionally connecting on the loveseat. The whole "we need to talk" conversation starter will only make a husband avoid his wife, so it's important to think about what language will resonate with him the best and help him open up to you.

Your husband wants to feel close to you, but the primary way most men feel closeness to their wife is through sex. As women, our primary way to feel close to our husband is through conversation, and the intimacy we feel through these talks often leads us to want to be more physically intimate as well. The best way to get your husband's attention is to tell him that you want to be closer to him and that you feel closest to him when he opens up to you emotionally about the ups and downs of his day—his hopes, his dreams. Tell him that your need for him to emotionally connect with you is as strong as his need to connect sexually, and he will have a better understanding.

It's important that we approach the issue in the right setting as well. For example, you're probably not going to get the best response out of your husband right when he gets home from work and his mind is reeling from the day. He doesn't want to feel ambushed. It's also a good rule of thumb not to call him out for not being emotionally available when the two of you are having a disagreement. The best time to talk about this issue is when the two of you are alone and settled, like right before bed, on a date night, or during a lunch date.

Recent research also suggests that men are more prone to having deeper conversations while doing an activity and when they are side by side with someone, as opposed to face to face. Isn't that fascinating? This doesn't mean that you and your husband should only have side-by-side conversations from now on, but it does mean that you might get a better listening ear from him if you approach his lack of emotional availability while on a walk, while driving somewhere, or when the two of you are working out together.

With that said, the most important thing to remember is not to ignore the problem and expect things to just fix themselves. Emotional neglect is a real thing, and it's heartbreaking. We can't have the vibrant and thriving marriage that God wants us to have when we refuse to connect emotionally. Lack of emotional connection creates a sterile and lifeless home life that is unsustainable and damaging.

If you're reading this and you feel like you've tried your best to approach your husband in a disarming way and have addressed his lack of emotional availability to no avail, please know that there is still hope for you. My friend, Janny, was in this predicament. She felt like she had tried everything she could to connect with her husband, but his long hours and lack of interest in her and their home life was tearing her heart apart. She also found herself in the negative habit of making a list of things to discuss with him the minute he got home from work. This only made things worse. It made him want to escape more and Janny felt even more unloved and unappreciated. So, she asked to him to go to counseling, and he attended—reluctantly.

It took several months, but eventually, he began to see that he needed to do a better job of being emotionally available for Janny. As suggested by the counselor, he also read a marriage book that helped him to realize that Janny wasn't asking for too much in needing him to connect with her. He had always thought that she was much "needier" than most wives. What he found when he read and talked with the counselor was that Janny wasn't needy at all; she just wanted to be close to him. She simply wanted to connect with him through conversation, laughter, and time together.

So, little by little, Janny's husband made more of an effort in their relationship. He stopped working late so he could come home and engage with Janny and the kids. He decided to finally take some time off work so he could take Janny and the kids on several vacations after years of excuses for why they didn't "need" to have a vacation. He started taking Janny on regular dates where they could talk without having to manage the kids. Needless to say, it was a huge shift for the better in their marriage, and they both feel closer than ever before. Now they are together in the loveseat.

If you currently feel emotionally disconnected from your spouse, please know that all hope is not lost. You can have the close, thriving marriage that you long for. Keep on fighting for and investing in your marriage, and your connection will grow stronger!

Dave

Some of you may be wondering how one can stay in the loveseat when one spouse is a believer and the other isn't? I recently had the opportunity to meet one of my favorite authors, Lee Strobel. He's written dozens of books about the Christian faith including the bestseller *The Case for Christ*, which was made into a movie. The book (and the film) tell the extraordinary story of Lee's life and his marriage.

Lee was an atheist and a successful journalist, so when his wife, Leslie, found a church and became a Christian, Lee thought she had lost her mind. He decided to use his journalism skills to research the Christian faith in an attempt to disprove it. However, the facts he found convinced him that Jesus is real, and the Bible is true.

But during those turbulent years, Lee and Leslie struggled in their marriage when Leslie was wholeheartedly following Christ and Lee was doing everything he could to undermine her faith. Ultimately, Leslie's powerful testimony of love and grace, combined with the evidence of Christianity, led Lee to give his heart to Christ and to devote the rest of his life to ministry. Decades later, Lee and Leslie have a wonderful marriage and a solid partnership in their faith and their ministry.

Many couples are in the situation Lee and Leslie once faced. It can cause tremendous stress on a marriage when one spouse has a devout faith in Christ and the other spouse doesn't. In that situation, they're operating from two different worldviews, and it makes unity in marriage and joining one another on the loveseat an elusive struggle. We often get questions from desperate husbands and wives who want to know how to connect with their unbelieving spouse.

I was talking with a lady at our church on Sunday and with tears in her eyes, she started to tell me about these same struggles in her marriage. With a trembling voice, she said, "My marriage is falling apart. You might not have even known that I'm married because my husband never comes to church with me. He's not a Christian. It's like we live on two different planets. Our value systems, beliefs, and worldviews are miles apart. My faith is the most important part of my life, but I can't share it with him, because when I do, he just accuses me of preaching at him. I feel like we keep drifting further and further apart. I pray about it every day and I do everything in my power to improve our relationship, but nothing seems to work. What should I do?"

This is one of the biggest marital challenges Ashley and I see. God knew this scenario could create a lot of heartaches, so He gives explicit warnings in the Scriptures for a believer not to marry a nonbeliever. No matter how much chemistry and compatibility you might think you have with someone, if one of you is a Christian and one is not, don't get married. God's commands are always for our protection.

But once you're already married, you can't build a time machine, so the Bible's instructions on whom to marry (or not to marry) don't apply. The Bible has specific instructions for this situation as well. I'm going to put the most direct passage of Scripture on this matter below and then unpack practical ways I believe every Christian should respond when married to a non-

Christian:

> *Now, I will speak to the rest of you, though I do not have a direct command from the Lord. If a fellow believer has a wife who is not a believer and she is willing to continue living with him, he must not leave her. And if a believing woman has a husband who is not a believer and he is willing to continue living with her, she must not leave him. For the believing wife brings holiness to her marriage, and the believing husband brings holiness to his marriage. Otherwise, your children would not be holy, but now they are holy. (But if the husband or wife who isn't a believer insists on leaving, let them go. In such cases, the believing husband or wife is no longer bound to the other, for God has called you to live in peace.) Don't you wives realize that your husbands might be saved because of you? And don't you husbands realize that your wives might be saved because of you?*
> 1 Corinthians 7:12–16 (NLT)

I believe every Christian who is married to a nonbeliever should do their very best to promote peace in an effort to be on the loveseat together. According to this passage of Scripture, you shouldn't pick fights with your spouse. And never use guilt, manipulation, or demands to get them to see things from your perspective. Jesus said,

> *"Blessed are the peacemakers"*
> Matthew 5:9

Strive to be the one who resolves conflicts in your marriage—not the one who starts them.

Lee Strobel said Leslie's life became some of the most compelling evidence for Christianity. The most powerful "sermons" come through actions and not just words. You are probably not going to talk your husband/wife into becoming a Christian, but your actions can make your faith seem so attractive that he/she might become interested. Even if they never accept Christ, your home is still going to have more peace and joy if you're living out a Christian example of love and grace.

As a Christian, you're called to love above all else. So, don't try to fix, change, or judge your spouse. Just love them. The rest is God's business. Remember, love is patient and kind (1 Corinthians 13:4), so be patient and kind toward your spouse. You will never be held accountable for the decisions that your spouse ultimately makes, but you will be held accountable for how you love him or her. Don't try to change your spouse— just love them. Love is the primary tool God uses to change us all.

Finally, pray and remember that God loves you and He loves your spouse. Prayer is powerful, and it always brings results. Sometimes God uses prayer to change our circumstances, and sometimes He uses prayer to simply change our perspective about our circumstances. Pray for your spouse daily. Pray for his/her salvation. Pray that God would help you to love him/her selflessly. Pray that God would give you strength, grace, and encouragement on those days when you feel alone in your marriage. Remember that Jesus is with you and He's never going to leave you or forsake you. And whether or not your spouse is in the loveseat with you or sitting in the *me* seat, trust God and remain faithful in prayer in the loveseat. You are never alone when God is with you!

Ashley

Now, I want to clarify that being on the loveseat with your spouse doesn't mean you lose your unique, God-designed individuality. Instead, it strengthens how God made you. Many of us are familiar with the iconic line, "You complete me" from the famous movie *Jerry Maguire*. I loved watching the tear-filled scene as Tom Cruise's character, Jerry, professed his undying need to be made whole by Renee Zellweger's character, Dorothy. It seemed to make perfect sense—two halves becoming one whole. But it's not at all how marriage is described in the Bible.

Marriage is in part a physical, sexual union between a husband and wife, but I love how Mark 10:8 records Jesus describing this connection even further: "For this reason a man will leave his father and mother and be united to his wife, and the two will become one flesh" (NIV). Jesus described the man and woman as the "two," not the "halves." He describes two individuals becoming one in mind, body, and spirit. When we marry our spouse, we are *uniting with* each other and proceeding to live life as two people with one covenant and mission. I may be splitting hairs here, but that means something to me.

As a young Christian woman, I longed to be married, and I prayed daily for my future spouse. I truly believe that God over-delivered when He gave me the greatest gift in my husband, Dave. He is my best friend, my lover, my comic relief, my cuddle partner, the best daddy ever, and much more. He is everything to me, but he does not complete me—he's not supposed to.

Before we met each other and eventually married, we were two, whole, single people. Both of us desired to be married, but we didn't see ourselves as half of a person. God can and will complete you. The emptiness we sometimes feel way down deep in our hearts comes from our sinful nature. It's the abandonment of God that Adam and Eve committed so long ago, but God did not abandon us. He sent Jesus to die on the cross for our sins. God bridged the gap, and only Jesus can fill the void in our heart. Only Jesus can make us complete.

If you feel that you are lacking something in your heart, please don't look to your spouse to fill it. Yes, we need tremendous love and support from each other every day, and we should offer it every single day. However, our spouse cannot complete us. He or she doesn't have the power to make us whole. Jesus does.

Who we marry is one of the most important decisions we can and will ever make. As husbands and wives, we play an essential role in each other's lives. However, our spouse cannot make us whole. A spouse has the power to lift our spirits with encouragement or bring us down with harsh criticism. He/she is our partner through the good times and bad times. He/she is our shoulder to cry on, best person to make us laugh, and more. But he/she doesn't have the power to fill a God-size void in our hearts.

This doesn't make our marriages any less romantic or intimate. I honestly find this to be good news because it places us on common ground, instead of hollow, glass pedestals. As human beings, we are flawed and sometimes fickle, and when we don't have a relationship with Jesus Christ, our void is magnified.

So, if you are trying to fill the void in your spouse's heart, or if you are expecting your spouse to fill the role of God in your life, I encourage you to turn to God. If you don't know Him yet, try talking to Him. You don't have to use any special language or try to be someone that you are not. Close your eyes and pray. God made you—*He knows you.* He loves you, and when you fully surrender to Him and accept the amazing gift of forgiveness that God has given you through the death and resurrection of His one and only son, Jesus Christ, you will finally find the wholeness you have been searching for. This doesn't mean that you will never feel lonely or sad, but it does mean that you have a relationship with your Maker. He is the One who can make you complete. Even if we are the only spouse in the *loveseat* and our spouse is in the *me* seat, we are never alone. God is with us. In fact, God Himself *is* the loveseat, because God *is* love. When a husband and wife are in the loveseat together, they aren't standing on their own feet; they are sinking into the loveseat together and trusting God to hold them up. They are resting in His love and counting on His strength to hold them together.

Dave

Ashley and I recently received a message on Facebook from a wife who is feeling frustrated, discouraged, and hopeless in a marriage where both spouses are in the *me* seats. She shared, "I don't know what to do anymore. My husband and I used to be best friends. We used to be in love. I don't know what changed or when it changed, but now it feels like we're just roommates. We're just two strangers sharing a house and sharing bills and sharing kids, but this isn't what I wanted our marriage to be. I'm not sure how to get back to what we had before. I can't keep going on like this. What do I do?"

This predicament keeps her awake at night and makes her days much more difficult than they need to be. Her struggle is tragic, but it's not unique. In our work with married couples from all over the world, we've seen a startling trend of marriages facing similar struggles, where both the husband and wife are in the *me* seats and the marriage is suffering. This is what Ashley and I call *the roommate trap*.

The roommate trap isn't like a mousetrap that snaps you in an instant. It's slow and methodical like an elaborate maze. Once a couple enters the maze of life's busyness (work, kids, bills), they find themselves wandering around and getting separated from one another. It's not an intentional separation; it's just what can happen when life is moving too fast.

In the maze, a couple gets into a kind of "autopilot" and they only join in the loveseat to talk business before retreating back to the *me* seats. Again, it doesn't happen all at once and it's rarely an intentional choice to pull away from each other. It's *subtle*. After a long season of just trying to keep their heads above water, one or both spouses begin to notice that the marriage isn't what it used to be. They're no longer best friends and lovers. There's an absence of meaningful conversation and laughter filling the home, and the silence is deafening. There's very little (if any) physical affection, and sex is nowhere on the radar. They act like roommates and nothing more. Sadly, they've fallen into the roommate trap.

When you're struggling in your marriage or feeling alone and isolated, it's easy to want to assign blame to the other spouse. It's also easy to blame yourself. Neither of these options are helpful. Instead of blaming, communicate with your spouse about what you're feeling. Ask him/her how they are feeling. Start to create some action-oriented steps to bring you both to the loveseat.

When couples tell me, "Things were so much better back when we were dating," I usually smile and ask, "Well, then why did you stop dating?" I'm trying to make the point that the dating, romance, and pursuit that happens early in a relationship shouldn't stop just because a couple marries. Sure, there are practical challenges when kids and bills come along, but there are also beautiful blessings in every season of marriage. You shouldn't try to recreate the early days of your marriage, because the current days can be even better, but you *can* start doing some of the positive things you did at the beginning of the relationship like staying up late just to talk, laughing over a movie together, sending love notes, or flirting with each other. All of these are great ways to help you and your spouse to grow closer and stay connected on the loveseat.

Ashley and I are convinced that prayer is one of the most intimate acts a married couple can share. When you pray for your spouse, it changes your perspective about them, and it brings you closer to him/her. Also, when you pray with your spouse, it simultaneously brings you closer to God and closer to each other. No marriage problem is bigger than God and when you invite the peace of Christ and the wisdom of the Holy Spirit into your marriage, transformation happens. When you don't know which way to turn, turn to Jesus and you'll be headed in the right direction—out of the *me* seats and into the loveseat with your spouse.

We live in a culture that teaches us to quit the moment something becomes difficult or uncomfortable. Many people are more committed to their diets, their hobbies, or their exercise routines than they are committed to their marriages. When your marriage is in a tough spot, refuse to give up. Keep fighting for each other and not against each other. You will get through this, and overcoming the struggle will make your marriage even stronger if you commit to staying in the loveseat with your spouse. It's worth it!

Ashley

What is the hardest challenge in your marriage? Think about that question for a minute. Your answer says a lot about the current state of your relationship. For Dave and me, the answer to that question has changed through the different seasons of our marriage. At one point it was financial stress. At another point it was managing complex family dynamics. At different points in marriage, we've wrestled with cross-country moves, depression, debt, parenting stress, work stress, health issues, and many other challenges along the way. We've come to realize that struggles are always a part of marriage because struggles are always a part of life. But it's how you choose to face those struggles that have a tremendous impact on the health of your marriage.

Recently, Dave and I had a conversation with a man at church who had been married for fifty years. His words profoundly changed our perspective on struggles in marriage. He and his wife have walked through many struggles and many seasons of life in their half century together. Their current struggles include a move from their hometown to be closer to family and a diagnosis of early Alzheimer's in his wife. Watching her battle dementia and lose her memories has clearly been one of the greatest struggles in their marriage, but apparently, not his biggest struggle, currently.

His wife was on a weekend trip with their daughter spending some "girl time" together. Dave and I asked him how he had been doing and he said, "Honestly, I'm not doing so well."

We didn't say it aloud, but we thought, *Of course you're not! You are in a new town trying to learn a new routine and you are having to watch your wife slowly lose her memories and her personality through the cruel disease of Alzheimer's. Nobody in your shoes would be doing well!*

What he said next left us speechless. When he was talking about why he was having such a hard time, his struggles had nothing to do with the factors we thought he meant. He said, "I'm having such a hard time because I love having her here with me. It has been years since I've had to go two days in a row without seeing her. I can't wait until she gets home tomorrow!"

While so many couples seem to try and invent ways to escape from each other, this man and his wife had created a relationship that neither spouse ever wanted to be without the other. They were rooted together on the loveseat—in sickness and in health—through all of life's challenges. In fact, even the thought of being apart left him feeling sick. This temporary distance, not the Alzheimer's or anything else, was his current greatest struggle in marriage. He simply *missed* his wife.

His perspective was an inspiring reminder to Dave and me that a marriage isn't defined by the size of your struggles but by the size of your commitment to overcome those struggles together. He felt he could face anything with his bride by his side and with their united faith in God and each other. No matter what life throws your way, your marriage will be able to survive any storm if you face it hand in hand and side by side on the loveseat with your spouse.

When life is hard, and marriage seems to be more difficult than usual, our feelings will change. However, our commitment to the loveseat—to unity—can be unwavering when we choose to stay committed through thick and thin. That is precisely why the *world's* view of love is not enough. But love, as God designed it, is all we need. We can't choose our feelings—we are human. But you can choose to love your spouse and to be committed to them no matter what. This is how marriage is supposed to work. The marriage thrives when both partners choose to love each other by staying committed to one another in the loveseat each and every day.

Love does for a marriage what breathing does for lungs, so do everything in your power to keep the love alive! Make time together a priority. Invest in your friendship with one another. Seek new ways to serve each other's needs. Through your words and your actions, consistently communicate your love, adoration, and commitment to one another. Friends, let's strive for that kind of rock-solid marriage—a love and commitment that will never fail.

8

NAKED FORGIVENESS

Dave

We all want to be the best we can be, but one factor that often holds people back from forgiving themselves or others is the nagging disappointment of how life has turned out for them so far. Many of us start out wide eyed and optimistic that our dreams for marriage will come true. We paint a picture of a marriage filled with success and happiness.

Reality in adulthood rarely measures up to the idealized dreams we had in childhood. As a kid, I had plans to be a professional athlete, a billionaire, and president of the United States. So far, none of those have happened. Instead of dwelling on how I've failed to live up to my childhood fantasies, I am learning to look at the picture God is painting with my life, as I extend forgiveness toward myself and others. It may not look like what I had in my head, but in light of eternity, the picture God is painting is something far more meaningful.

A few years ago, my perspective on this changed in a single night. It all began with a trip to Walmart. God definitely has a sense of humor. Only He could bring a life-changing moment out of a trip to Walmart.

Our family was preparing for the Christmas season, and we were loading up on our usual groceries while simultaneously trying to distract our kids from all the breakable items. Several months earlier, one of our kids had knocked over an end-of-aisle wine display leaving broken glass and red wine spilled all over the floor. I had been attempting to avoid contact with all

ᅟ

ᅠᅠᅠᅟ

ᅠ

ᅠ ᅠᅠ

Walmart employees ever since. I strongly believed they had a picture of our family on the "Most Wanted Criminals" board in the employee break room.

On this day, our kids managed not to break anything, but we did end up buying more than I was planning to buy. That seems to happen every time for some reason. One of the unexpected purchases came when we passed a display of gingerbread house kits.

My kids immediately started their begging. Normally, I have the strength to resist their pleas because if they had their way, the cart would be filled to the brim with Twinkies and toys. This request caught my attention because as I looked at the box, I envisioned a magical evening. The kids squealed with delight when I granted their request. We were going to make a gingerbread house!

My mind created a scene from a Charles Dickens novel as our family cheerfully assembled and decorated the gingerbread house. There would be Christmas music playing in the background, eggnog, and good cheer. At some point, one of my children would say with Tiny Tim's British accent, "God bless us, every one!"

We bought the kit, but on the way home, the boys started fighting over the box. We weren't setting the tone for the magical Christmas evening I'd envisioned. I loudly threatened to pull the minivan over on several occasions during the short drive home. Visions of sugarplums were no longer dancing through my head.

When we arrived at the house and emptied out the contents of the box, the pieces of the gingerbread house were *all* broken. Not one piece was intact. I was so disappointed. I had just wasted eight dollars. That's a lot of money for gingerbread. After expressing my frustration with the kids, I started pouting like a spoiled toddler.

Ashley is so much more patient than I am. She came over to me and asked what was wrong. I thought the answer was pretty obvious, but I tried not to sound condescending in my response. "It's broken! It's ruined!"

She smiled and gently replied, "It's not ruined."

I looked at her like she was crazy, and in frustration I held up the box and replied, "Of course it's ruined! It's never going to look like the picture on the box."

What she said next completely changed my thinking. In her patience and wisdom, she was about to teach me a lesson much more valuable than my eight-dollar purchase. She said, "It doesn't have to look like the picture on the box."

Think about that statement. So much of my frustration in life comes from unmet expectations. I'll bet it's the same in your life too. I paint a picture in my mind of how a situation should play out, and if the end result doesn't look exactly like my mental masterpiece, then I walk away disappointed. But imagine what could happen if we allowed God to create a masterpiece even with the broken pieces. We didn't end up with an actual gingerbread house, but we had some amazing, oddly shaped gingerbread cookies. They were delicious.

We laughed more that night than we had in a long time. We were covered in icing and crumbs by the end of it, but it was well worth the mess. I almost missed out on that moment because the rigidity of my expectations didn't make room for the beautiful spontaneity of the opportunity. I'm so thankful my wife had more vision than I had.

When our lives or our marriages don't look like the picture-perfect images we imagined, we can be faced with weighty sadness, self-defeat, or unforgiveness. Maybe your life or marriage doesn't look anything like the perfect picture on the box, but it doesn't have to. God loves you and your spouse right where you are. He's the only perfect part of our lives, and He wants to create something beautiful with the broken pieces of your hearts and lives—if you let Him.

The same is true for our marriages. If we allow an unrealistic view of marriage to take root in us, then we may be tempted to have bitterness or unforgiveness in our hearts toward our spouse. Do you have broken pieces in your marriage? Do you have shards of dreams that feel broken? God can heal you and your marriage. You simply need to invite Him. Don't miss the opportunities God has for your marriage. God has blessings hidden in your broken pieces.

Maybe your marriage doesn't look like the picture on the box right now. Perhaps you struggle with deep disappointment over the way your marriage relationship has developed up to this point in your story. Whatever your current circumstances may be, look at your marriage through the lens of God's love for you and your spouse. His love for you is limitless, and His plan for your marriage is *good*.

Ashley

Every marriage goes through difficult seasons. Some are harder than others. There will be times when we let each other down. But it's in those moments that we need to do our best to forgive one another as quickly as we can. This won't be easy, but it is necessary to pursue healing and restoration.

Forgiving someone doesn't mean that we are saying what they did is okay or that it didn't hurt us; it just means that we are willing to move forward and pursue healing over retaliation. Forgiveness is a choice, and both spouses must actively choose to forgive one another each and every day. When we do this, more peace and understanding will be present in our marriage and family.

As much as we talk about confession and forgiveness within the church, I believe we often fail to apply it in the context of our marriages, because let's be honest, it's a hard task! The idea of being vulnerable and sharing your weaknesses and shortcomings with another person can be a really hard pill to swallow—which is precisely why God calls us to do it. The practice of laying down our pride in the act of confession opens the door for the opportunity to forgive, which is the sacred glue that holds marriages together.

Apologizing and extending forgiveness are essential to culti-vating a healthy marriage, but what should one do when a spouse refuses to apologize for broken trust or wrongdoing in the marriage? When a spouse refuses to apologize, it absolutely breaks the other spouse's heart. It makes them feel disrespected, unloved, and unimportant. Over time, this refusal to admit wrongdoing creates a huge wedge between a husband and wife. So, what can a spouse do to encourage his/her spouse to apologize?

It starts with appealing to the heart. Sometimes, a spouse may not apologize because they simply don't know that what they did was wrong. In these cases, we must go to our spouse and explain how the behavior made us feel. For example, if you discover that your spouse has been keeping a secret from you that they didn't seem to think was a big deal, you must explain how this made you feel betrayed and deceived. Tell your spouse that even though there was no malicious intent, it still hurt you.

It's important to remember that any time we end up hurting our spouse's feelings or hinder their trust in us—even when we didn't mean to or don't agree that hurt feelings or loss of trust are warranted—we must be willing and quick to apologize without any excuses. It's also important to remember that we must be quick to forgive our apologetic spouse and not hold grudges and growing resentment against them. This keeps the peace and shows that we care about how our spouse feels while fostering an open line of communication.

What if a spouse is quick to verbally apologize, but makes no real changes in behavior? To be honest, this is a difficult spot to be in, so it requires some tough love and hard conversations. First of all, we must lovingly, but pointedly, call our spouse out on it. Tell them that you are thankful for the verbal apologies, but their lack of effort to change is only hurting your heart and relationship even more. If this kind of behavior becomes perpetual, an effective next step would be attending a crisis marriage retreat and/or seeing a Christian counselor on a regular basis.

Sometimes the spouse who won't make changes is caught in a stronghold or sin that cannot be stopped on their own. Things like addiction, inappropriate relationships, gambling, and other secret-led lifestyles can be gripping and transform someone into an unabashedly prideful and hateful person. This can certainly wreak havoc in a marriage. It is important for the healthy person to get their spouse the help they need to get well.

Sometimes an unapologetic spouse simply views apologizing as a sign of weakness, so they avoid apologies at all costs. This is terribly unhealthy and hurtful and it's important for this spouse to change their perception. Apologizing is a healthy and powerful part of communication, and it cannot be one sided in a marriage. If your spouse struggles with apologizing, try to have an open conversation with them about their own experiences with apologies and forgiveness.

Tell your spouse about your own. These kinds of *naked* conversations can lead to a better understanding about why your spouse is so resistant to saying, "I'm sorry," and it will help you to explain why your spouse's resistance to apologies hurts you so deeply. If your spouse seems to shut down when you try to have these open and honest talks, then it might be time to go see a Christian marriage counselor to help lead the conversation.

In the meantime, keep praying for your spouse. God is with you and for you. He sees your hurting heart and He longs for your spouse to make things right just as much, if not more, than you do. Don't give up. Keep having those hard conversations with your spouse in the most loving way you can, and resist arguing about it. Get the help that you both need and please know that God loves you and has an amazing plan for your life. He uses all struggles—even difficult marital ones—for our good and His glory. He is our ever-present help in time of need, and

He will get you both through this and bring peace, joy, and understanding to your marriage.

Dave

While forgiveness is important, I think marriages would be better off by simply avoiding the offense in the first place. Some of you might be wondering what I mean by this. Well, I'm going to make a confession to you. It's a confession many men will try to deny, but it's the truth. Here it is—we men get our feelings hurt a lot more than we admit. We are not nearly as tough as we pretend to be. Wow! I already feel a sense of relief now that this huge secret is off my chest!

People tend to create gender stereotypes where women are more *emotional*, but both men and women are emotional beings. Yes, women often are more outwardly demonstrative with their emotional expression while men tend to internalize, but both genders get their feelings hurt at about the same rate.

Sometimes, we hurt each other on purpose (which is never justified), but often in marriage, a husband and wife can hurt each other's feelings by accident. When this happens, forgiveness is needed. Below are a few examples of the primary ways women unknowingly hurt their husband.

For example, a wife can unknowingly and unintentionally hurt her husband's feelings when she double-checks or corrects his work on simple tasks. Men tend to gain great pride through their work. Even with simple tasks like mowing the yard, most of us guys take great pride in a job well done. When a wife is always checking or correcting a husband's work around the house or yard, she just thinks she is helping him see his blind spots (which she probably is), but often this causes deep frustration or even hurt in the husband. He may not vocalize it, but it can turn into an outburst of frustration in other areas. If a man thinks nothing he does is ever good enough for his wife, it will crush his spirit.

Another way a wife may unintentionally hurt her man is by

consistently rejecting his sexual advances. Most men list sex as their number one or number two need in marriage (it's not anywhere in the top five for most women). Since a man's wife is the only legitimate place where this need can be met, when there's consistent *rejection* it will not only create physical frustration, it can also create some emotional pain. Any form of rejection in marriage will eventually create some hurt feelings.

Another way an offense may happen is when the wife consistently expresses desire for things the family budget can't afford. One of the biggest desires of most men is to provide for the needs and wants of his wife and family. When a wife makes comments lamenting the family's limited resources or how she'd love to buy something far beyond the family's current budget, even though she means no harm, most men will internalize these comments and think, *I'm a loser. I can't give my wife what she wants.* It's okay to want things and work toward having more but choosing an attitude of contentment and resourcefulness in marriage is key for both spouses.

Sometimes offenses happen when the wife doesn't say thank you because she assumes her husband knows he's appreciated. As mentioned earlier, men desire to hear the phrase "thank you" even more than they desire to hear "I love you." Both genders have a need to feel appreciated, but men tend to link gratitude with respect and men tend to value respect and appreciation in the way that most women tend to value love and affection. Choose to celebrate the best in him instead of pointing out the worst in him. Saying, "thank you" or "I really appreciate all you do for us" to your husband as often as you can will not only prevent offenses from taking root, it will also encourage him to keep working to become the husband of your dreams. Sometimes the best road to reconciliation is to avoid the offense in the first place.

Ashley

In marriage, there will be times when you "step on each other's toes" so to speak, but the really hurtful moments happen when you "step on each other's hearts" and wound your spouse on an emotional level. There are times when one spouse might intentionally try to hurt the other, but Dave and I are convinced that many of the most damaging wounds in marriage are inflicted unintentionally. And again, like Dave wrote, the best way to walk out forgiveness in your marriage is to avoid the offense in the first place. So how do we do that? I believe it's through healthy communication.

Healthy communication is essential to a thriving marriage, but it takes work. Without realizing it, we can be careless with our words and actions and inadvertently hurt our spouse's feelings, needing forgiveness as a result. When our feelings are hurt, we are less likely to communicate in a productive and kind way. We get caught in the negative spiral of assuming the worst of each other, and every discussion becomes a fight.

How can a husband avoid the marriage trap of unintentionally hurting his wife's feelings? One way is by not speaking harshly to your wife or saying negative things about her in public. This one is so important, and it usually stems from bad communication habits that develop over time in marriage. We must never speak harshly to our spouse or talk rudely about our spouse—even if we feel like we are justified. We must treat each other with respect both inside and outside the walls of our home. Harsh words build giant walls between us and make us feel unloved and insignificant.

Husbands, if you tend to yell at your wife or use derogatory words toward her, please stop immediately. There is a better way. You can stop this negative cycle by choosing to focus on the good and speaking in a loving tone toward her. Dave has so wisely said, "The tone of your words becomes the tone of your marriage."

If you are having trouble doing this, I highly suggest that you both invest time in working on your communication in your marriage. And if you have done this in the past, ask her for forgiveness.

Another way husbands unintentionally hurt their wives is by avoiding meaningful conversation with her. Many husbands avoid meaningful conversation with their wives simply because they feel like they are "out of words" for the day, but this is something that is important to your wife and it may take an extra effort on your part.

When your wife asks about your day, she isn't trying to interrogate you. She just wants to connect with you—all of you. She wants to know about everything—the good, the bad, and the ugly. The next time she asks you about your day, don't just say, "It was fine," and plop down in front of the TV with a Coke and corn chips. Engage with her. Look in her eyes and tell her what's on your heart. Listen as she tells you what's going on with her. This kind of daily conversation allows you both to have a better understanding of what's going on in each other's lives. Give her your best time and attention first, and this will help to avoid conflict later.

Making plans without talking to your wife first can be hurtful. My husband and I have talked to many couples who struggle with this issue, and it really comes down to one thing—*pride*. I've heard some husbands say, "Well, I'm a grown man. I shouldn't have to ask my wife if I can go somewhere." But when we marry, we become one. It's no longer *his* and *hers*, it's *ours*. And that includes our schedules. We must consider our spouse whenever we make plans.

It's as simple as saying, "Honey, some of the guys want to get together and watch the game this Wednesday night. Do you care if I go?" This one simple step of consulting her first will help your wife know that you consider her in all things and you respect her thoughts and opinions in all matters. Nine times out of ten, she will probably say, "Sure. Go ahead," but sometimes, she will remind you that you both already have something on the agenda. Either way, you are showing her love and respect by consulting with her first before making your own plans, and this will keep your marriage strong and avoid offenses.

Another important way for husbands to avoiding hurting their wives is by not fulfilling your own sexual needs using porn. I receive multiple messages every single day from wives who are broken-hearted after finding out that their husband has been watching porn. Friends, let me be crystal clear here—porn destroys marriages. Yet, so many husbands (even Christian husbands) struggle with this sin in secret.

You may tell yourself that it's harmless and that nobody is getting hurt, but that is a lie. Porn warps your mind to desire things that no one person can fulfill, and it makes you think that your spouse is less desirable and less sexually fulfilling. When you continue to go back to porn again and again and again, you stop initiating sex with your wife. Then she's left wondering why you never want her anymore. The two of you simply "exist" with a sexless marriage—all while you meet your own sexual needs with porn. Sound familiar?

Husbands, if this describes you, please know that you are not alone in this struggle, but it will tear you and your marriage apart if you don't stop this habit as soon as possible. She needs to know, and she can be a great help to you in providing encouragement and accountability in this process of healing.

The more intentional we are with our words and actions, the more our marriages will thrive. Husbands, think about each of these four things and do your very best to make the adjustments needed. When you do this, your wife will feel loved and respected by you, and your marriage will soar.

Dave

Recently, Ashley and I were walking off stage at a marriage conference when a distraught woman came up to us. With tears rolling down her cheeks, she told us that she needed prayer and guidance. Through her sobs, she shared a tragically familiar story. Her once-happy marriage had slowly been poisoned by pornography. Her husband had fallen deep into his addiction and now, what he had once seen as harmless entertainment, had stolen almost everything from him and shattered his wife's heart.

In our years of working with couples, we've watched pornography devastate marriages. In fact, we're convinced that there is no greater enemy of intimacy than pornography. We're also convinced that it's a secret among Christians that needs to be dragged out of the darkness and into the light.

Nearly every time someone approaches us with a marriage crisis, porn is part of the story. I vividly remember the moment when I finally understood how widespread this crisis has become, even in Christian marriages. Ashley and I were speaking at a marriage event at our church, but this time, instead of just sharing statistics, I wanted to help everyone visualize the real people behind the numbers.

I asked all the men to stand whose birthdays were in January, February, March, April, May, June, July, or August. These standing men made up approximately 62 percent of the total men in the room. According to Barna (the most trusted name in Christian statistics), 62 percent of men claim to be Christian and yet view pornography at least once a month. Let that sink in for a minute. 62 percent. That's a clear majority. It's nearly two out of three men.

I was shocked to see a real representation of this statistic with my own eyes. There were hundreds of men standing and I found myself speechless as I surveyed the crowd and reflected on the devastating statistic these men represented. The majority of Christian men are actively committing a mental form of infidelity by Jesus' own standard. He said,

> "To look at a woman lustfully is to commit adultery in your heart."
> Matthew 5:28 (NLT)

As the men stood all around me and I saw what 62 percent actually looks like, this staggering statistic became so much more than a number. I was looking at the faces of husbands, sons, fathers, and grandfathers. I was looking at faces of friends and leaders I know and respect. In that moment I realized the obvious truth that we are in the midst of a Christian porn crisis. Any form of lust is harmful. The objectification of human beings and extramarital fantasies create long-lasting scars in our minds, souls, and marriages.

I didn't need the studies to show me that porn is harmful. I knew it from personal experience. I was once part of that 62 percent. A secret porn habit haunted me from my teenage years into the early years of my marriage. There were long seasons where willpower would keep me away, but then I'd fall back into that same pit of sin and cycle of shame. I know from experience that porn is no more a form of entertainment than rat poison is a form of food.

I've seen the heartbreak in my bride's eyes when she discovered the awful truth. I've known the feeling of losing control of my thoughts because of the reels of filthy images that would play on repeat in my mind. I've known what it feels like to be addicted and trapped by porn. I have lived this story.

I have also lived a story of grace. I've known the forgiveness of a Savior who gave His life to set me free from all sin and shame. I've known the love and forgiveness of an amazing wife who helped me, even while healing from her own wounds that were caused by my sin. I've known redemption and freedom and you can too!

As followers of Christ and believers in God's sacred plan for marriage, I believe that all of us should be on this crusade together to get porn out of our lives and out of our marriages. The solutions are more complex than can be addressed in this book, but for starters, we need to be willing to call this a sin and repent of our use of it or our indifference to another's use of it.

We need to have healthy conversations about porn and purity in our churches, where tragically so many are suffering with this sin in silence while the church pretends it's not a problem. We need accountability from our spouse and from same-gender accountability relationships. We need transparency and trust in our marriages. We need to reclaim God's original and ever-perfect plan for sex and marriage.

If you are currently struggling with pornography, please know that you're not alone and there is help and hope available. Your first step is to confess your sin to your Savior and embrace His forgiveness. Next, confess your sin to your spouse and ask for their forgiveness. Work to rebuild the trust your actions have damaged. Actively pursue accountability and porn-blocking-and-tracking software on all your devices through services like Covenant Eyes or X3Watch. Finally, keep growing in your relationship with God and your relationship with your spouse. Your best days are ahead of you!

Ashley

Grace is the centerpiece of a healthy and thriving marriage. If a husband and wife keep score in the marriage or hold a grudge, they both lose. With that said, Dave and I believe that forgiveness and trust are two different things. You forgive instantly when your spouse has hurt you, but trust is different. Trust has to be earned, and it can only be earned through consistent trust-building actions. When you forgive your spouse, you are saying, "You hurt me, but I'm going to pursue reconciliation. I'm going to let go of the bitterness and move towards healing and restoration with you."

When Dave and I talk about *naked forgiveness,* it's not forgiveness with a clause attached. It's total forgiveness because that is how God forgives us. He forgives us over and over again. Whenever I share about Dave's past struggle with porn, people often ask me how I was able to forgive him. I respond that God *always* forgives me, so I'm called to do the same. And yes, Dave got caught up in sin that ultimately hurt me, but in order for our marriage to heal, I had to forgive him. If we say we forgive our spouse but we hold grudges or try to retaliate by constantly trying to make our spouse feel ashamed, it isn't really forgiveness.

Naked forgiveness has no strings attached. Naked forgiveness allows us to truly surrender our heartache and anger to God—believing that He is the one who can make things right and restore broken marriages. When we forgive, we forgive freely and expect God to do the rest.

I love what Colossians 3:13–14 says:

> *"Make allowance for each other's faults, and forgive anyone who offends you. Remember, the Lord forgave you, so you must forgive others. Above all, clothe yourselves with love, which binds us all together in perfect harmony."*
> *(NLT)*

One of the most popular TV movies in recent years was Lifetime's *The Client List*, which chronicled the true story of a Texas wife and mom who started making money by working as a prostitute. Her double life was finally brought to light when the brothel was raided by police and her secrets were exposed. Her husband was disgusted and shocked, and she was eventually abandoned by everyone she loved.

You might think that kind of crazy story line only happens on TV, but the Bible actually has a similar story, but with a much better ending. The Bible's version is about a man named Hosea with a wife named Gomer. Hosea loved his wife unconditionally, and that was put to the test when she abandoned her husband and family to return to her old life of prostitution.

By the time Hosea found out, they'd had several children, and he wasn't sure if any of them were his. To make matters even worse, her crimes had landed her in prison. Based on the laws of the day, her next step was to be sold into slavery to repay her debts. Hosea had every earthly right to write her off and leave her to the fate she had created for herself, but God had other plans. God wanted to use this whole situation to show the amazing grace and unimaginable love He has for us even in those moments when we are completely unworthy.

God moved Hosea's heart toward forgiveness and compassion. Hosea went to the slave auction and took most of his life's savings to purchase back his wife. Based on the culture's legal system, she now would have had no rights at all. He would have had all the power in the relationship, and he could have used it to punish her for the rest of her life. Knowing this, she bowed her head to him and called him *master*.

What happened next is one of the most beautiful displays of grace ever recorded. In essence, he looked at her and said, "Never call me your master. I am your husband." He gave up his rights to punish, control, or humiliate her; and instead, he welcomed her home as his wife. This simple but powerful act of forgiveness shows us what *naked forgiveness* really is. It is also a beautiful picture of the unmerited grace and love God offers to us all.

I'm not sure how trust has been broken in your marriage, and I'm definitely not advocating that you give your spouse a free pass to break your heart—a healthy relationship must be built on trust, accountability, mutual respect, and honesty. Our hope is simply that this story will open your mind and heart a little wider to let more love and grace flow into your marriage. If we deserved forgiveness or could earn it, then it wouldn't be called grace, which is a gift from the Lord. And grace is where all *naked forgiveness* must begin.

9

NAKED PURPOSE

Dave

A few mischievous friends and I were trying to carry out a century-old tradition by climbing into the steeple of our chapel on the campus of Georgetown College. We got lost in that big, dark building, so we never made it to the steeple, but we did find something that would forever change me.

Our misguided quest led us to a hidden door. We entered a dark room. Enough moonlight was trickling in through the old stained-glass windows for us to see that the room was full of something. My curiosity got the best of me, and I decided that I had to flip the light switch to see where we were, even if it meant we got caught trespassing.

As my eyes began to adjust to the light and the room came into focus, it took me a moment to comprehend what I was seeing. From floor to ceiling, from wall to wall, this room was packed full of a hundred years' worth of...trophies. There were trophies for music, academics, football, baseball, philanthropy, and everything else you can imagine.

These awards had once been raised in moments of celebration, but now they sat in a forgotten room. They represented accomplishment and sacrifice, but now they lay in broken pieces in dusty boxes. They didn't seem to matter at all.

A quote I'd heard from Dr. James Dobson rang in my ears, "Life will trash your trophies."

Standing in that forgotten room was a transformative experience for me. I decided I didn't want to spend my life chasing trophies that wouldn't really matter. I didn't want my life's achievements to be things that could be stuffed in a forgotten, dusty room.

Achievements and awards are nice, but the enduring treasures are our relationships—our *marriages*. Our marriages must always trump our trophies. Trophies can't love us back.

Don't neglect your spouse in pursuit of wealth or success. Any success you achieve at the expense of your marriage isn't really success. Live your life so that when you reach the end, you and your spouse will be stronger and closer because of the choices you made together. God wants us to have eternal perspective, which means we must live in the moment, while also considering the eternal legacy we want to leave.

God has a masterful purpose for our marriages. Making your spouse happy is wonderful, but God wants us to move beyond this desire to an even greater purpose—*being fruitful*. Marriage is an amazing opportunity for husbands and wives to leave an eternal impact on those around them. Marriage is not about us, it's about us bringing God's kingdom here on earth as it is in heaven. As we love one another, and together *love* others through our actions, then the world is changed. And ultimately, we are changed.

What do I mean by this? Well, Ashley and I believe that marriages should grow stronger with time. Couples should continue pursuing, encouraging, and adoring each other through all the seasons of the relationship. However, sometimes marriages get stuck in the ruts of daily monotony. One of the most effective ways to break out of a rut in your marriage is to selflessly serve. Jesus taught His disciples to *serve* one another. He gave them a practical example by washing their feet, one after the other, following their final meal together.

Serving creates an antidote to the toxicity of complacency in marriage. When a couple chooses to serve each other and the people around them, the marriage instantly improves. Recently, I read a story about a couple named Francis and Lisa Chan, who put this concept into practice in a beautiful and unique way. Francis Chan is a pastor who I've admired for years, and I was blown away by what he and his wife did to celebrate their twentieth wedding anniversary.

The Chans wanted to do something special to mark two decades of marriage. They looked into resorts around the globe, but then they decided to do something completely unconventional. Instead of going someplace where they could be served, they wanted to go someplace where they could serve others.

They bought two plane tickets to Africa and went to visit some missionaries they had been financially supporting. Francis and Lisa rolled up their sleeves and served food to hungry people, constructed shelters for homeless people, and worked alongside their missionary friends to free women who were trapped in a cycle of poverty and prostitution.

The couple had tears in their eyes as they shared this experience. It became one of the most extraordinary experiences of their lives. They came home from their life-changing anniversary trip and decided to write a book together putting their hearts on paper in *You and Me Forever: Marriage in Light of Eternity*. Every penny made from the sale of their book is being donated to the ministries in Africa where they served together for their twentieth anniversary.

When you and your spouse reach the end of your time on earth, what will matter most will be the moments you served each other and the moments you served alongside each other. When we remove selfishness from our marriages, love will be all that remains. That's the kind of love that can change your marriage and change the world through your marriage.

Wherever you are in your marriage, know that you can grow stronger. Any relationship left on autopilot will slowly drift toward atrophy, but any relationship given consistent investments of time, focus, and selfless service will flourish until the end. Your best days together can still be ahead of you and not behind you.

Ashley

The longer Dave and I are married, the more we see the power of the *fruitful* marriage. Loving God isn't just to make our lives and marriages better. I know that might sound a little funny, but let me explain. The more we love God, the more capacity we will have to love others. God wants us to make the world around us better as a result of our love. How do I know? Because that is the command God gave to the first married couple, Adam and Eve. After He created them, He blessed them and said, "Parah"—*be fruitful.*

One word has the power to change everything, and God is the creator of words. He spoke this world into existence just by using His words. As Dave and I have studied God's design for marriage, we wanted to go back to find out what God said to that very first married couple in the garden. And the first word God spoke to them was the Hebrew word *Parah.* Genesis 1:28a reads,

> *"Then God blessed them and said, 'Be fruitful and multiply.*
> *Fill the earth and govern it.'"*
> *(NLT)*

I think many of us have heard this verse and we can easily dismiss it, thinking God just wanted Adam and Eve to have a bunch of kids so they could populate the earth; however, God's first command wasn't *multiply*, it was *be fruitful.* This command through the word *Parah* has several meanings. God wants us to bear fruit in our individual lives and our marriages, to flourish as a couple, and to cause others around us to bear fruit as well.

Some of you see this word *fruitfulness* and you are wondering what this really means as it relates to your marriage. All through Scripture, God uses agricultural metaphors because back then everyone farmed. But in modern culture, we aren't as used to farming terms. And no, God doesn't want us to have more apples or bananas in our lives; instead, He wants us to have more fruits of the Spirit.

*"But the fruit of the Spirit is love, joy, peace, forbearance,
kindness, goodness, faithfulness, gentleness and self-control.
Against such things there is no law."*
Galatians 5:22–23 (NIV)

When God says He wants us to bear fruit (to *Parah*), He is
telling us to develop and cultivate more of these fruits in our
hearts, lives, homes, and marriages. More *love*. More *joy*. More
patience.

Imagine what our marriages would look like if we got rid of
the weeds and we had more of this Galatians type of fruit. This
is the picture of what God has for us. But these fruits of the
Holy Spirit only flow through our lives when we are rooted in
Christ.

For us to have healthy growth in our lives, there has to be
this element of pruning. As a couple you bear fruit when you
allow God to prune your heart and life for new growth. John
15:1 reads,

*"I am the true vine, and my Father is the vinedresser. Every
branch in me that does not bear fruit he takes away, and every
branch that does bear fruit he prunes, that it may bear more
fruit."*
(ESV)

I love to garden. Growing up, my mom and dad taught me
a lot about plants, so I love this imagery of gardening and
pruning. It's very real to me. In fact, when Dave and I lived in
Georgia, we had two big azalea bushes, and I was so excited to
work with them because I knew they have beautiful blooms in
the spring. One day during the fall, Dave came out to the front
yard and I was chopping away at these azalea bushes. I kind of
freaked him out because he didn't know what I was doing, and
here I was with these huge clippers just hacking away at our
bushes.

I must have looked like a crazy lady! Dave didn't know

what hedge clippers were, so to him it looked like something out of a horror movie as I attacked those bushes. I wasn't only cutting off the dead parts, but I was cutting off the live parts too. Again, Dave, not knowing anything about gardening, was like, "Sweetie, are you okay? Because you appear to be *killing* that poor helpless bush." I told him that cutting away the old growth is actually what encourages the plant to grow.

It seems counterintuitive. Why would you cut away at something to make it grow? And yet, that is exactly what does cause it to grow. This is imagery God gives us in Scripture, and imagery that every farmer and gardener understands, but it is also a powerful word picture that we are called to apply to our lives. In order for these azalea bushes to have those gorgeous blooms in the spring, I needed to prune them, and it was messy.

In fact, the bushes looked worse for a short time after, but this was the only way to ensure growth for the future. They had to be pruned. Sure enough, when spring came around, those azalea bushes were beautiful, and they had more blooms than the year before. I continued to prune my azalea bushes year after year to keep them healthy. In the same way, God wants to periodically prune our hearts—we just have to let Him.

God wants to prune our hearts so that we can be made new and bear more fruit. In order for us to make room for more growth in our lives, we need to allow God to prune our lives. He is the master gardener of our hearts and lives, and He knows what needs to be removed. Many times, as a couple, we kind of look at our spouse and think it's our job to prune our spouse. But it isn't.

Honestly, this happens a lot in marriage. We think we need to take the clippers and start chopping away at our spouse with our invisible pruning shears. We can have this idea, "Well, God calls us to prune so I'm putting these clippers on you!" We do this through our criticism, through comments like, "You never do this right," or "You always let me down." *Ouch*! Not a good idea. We think we are helping but all we are doing is creating a bloodbath. God never calls us to prune each other. Only God is the master gardener who prunes with a surgeon-like scalpel, so we come out *better* through the heart pruning process. God doesn't ask a husband and wife to prune each other because that only causes hurt and pain; instead, He calls us both to essentially take one handle each of the pruning shears so that *together* we can prune our lives—our schedules, our finances, our pace, etc.

Dave

Ashley and I believe one of the biggest *weeds* choking marriages right now is—busyness. A lot of times couples have good intentions, but their marriages are being suffocated by insanely busy schedules. Our lives have become overly busy, and if Satan can't outright bust up your marriage, then he is content to push you too fast, run you ragged, and deplete you of the energy and focus you need to invest in your marriage.

A lot of us are going too fast. We need to slow down to the rhythm of life that God modeled for us in Genesis when He rested after bringing forth His Creation. Sabbath rest is something that marriages need in order to remain healthy. When God rested on the seventh day, He modeled for us this rhythm that is sustainable, enjoyable, and one that makes room for growth and for relationships to flourish.

Often in marriage we get busy with our kids' activities, work, volunteering, and things that we keep saying yes to. However, we never stop doing the things that are already on our schedules because we think, *It's all good stuff so I need to keep doing it.* The bad stuff is easy to see and prune away, but what about the good stuff? We need to have the discipline to prune away some good things out of our lives too.

Ashley and I have come to realize that a lot of times we have to cut out some good things in our lives to make room for better things—like growth. As a couple, each of you needs to take hold of the pruning shears and together you must prune your schedules. Evaluate where you are and set a vision of where you want to be. Many times, we can say yes to a lot of good things, but that keeps you from the *best* things for your marriage. Busyness is the enemy of peace. We need to be willing to prune away some of our activities in order to produce more fruits of peace in our lives and fewer weeds of chaos.

Early in our marriage, we were running ragged. We were trying to stay on top of our commitments, while running our children around to their different activities. It was exhausting. Finally, when we stopped to evaluate where we were at as a couple and a family, we realized we weren't having family dinners together as often because we were always on the run. We felt disconnected as a family and we knew we needed to prune some things. We decided that we were doing a lot of good things, but it wasn't *good* when we did them all at the same time. So, we pruned our schedules by putting some of our activities on the shelf for a different season.

We did this with our kids' schedules too, letting them pick one activity to be in at a time, instead of multiple activities. And for us, with four boys, this made a huge difference for our schedule as a family. Find what works for your family and be willing to prune your schedule. This takes both spouses working together and not directing those shears at each other, but at your schedules instead.

For pruning schedules, my dad gave me the best advice—a happy wife is a happy life. When Ashley and I were days away from our wedding, my wise dad said, "Son, always invest the best of yourself into your marriage. Put your wife ahead of yourself. Strive to make her a happy woman. A happy wife creates a happy life." My parents have a wonderful marriage. They love each other, and they actually like each other too, so I took Dad's advice to heart. I've found it to be completely true. When Ashley is happy—I'm happy.

Now, you might be asking, "How can I make my wife happy?" That's a great question and a complicated one because

I don't think it's possible for one person to make another person happy. In fact, when we expect a spouse to make us happy, both spouses usually end up *unhappy*. A lot of marriages struggle because both spouses blame each other for their unhappiness. Still, I've learned there are some specific ways a husband can cultivate a garden of happiness and joy for his wife.

Ashley and I, during a busy season in our marriage, had the opportunity to take on a project that would instantly bring a good amount of additional income. Immediately, I wanted to do it! I was already mentally spending the extra money. The problem is that the stress and strain of this project was going to fall mostly on Ashley. She was already working hard in so many areas and she didn't have the extra margin to take on a new project.

She saw that I was excited about the opportunity, so to be supportive and encouraging to me, she agreed to do it. She's always willing to support me (even when my ideas are bad). As we started making preparations to begin the project, I sensed the stress she was feeling. She insisted she was okay and willing to take on the extra workload, but I knew she didn't have peace about it.

I made the decision to pull the plug. I knew that no amount of extra money would be worth taking joy or peace away from her. I told her that I didn't want to do the project because I would much rather have the extra peace, joy, and time in our home, instead of the extra money and stress. I could see the weight of that stress lift off her shoulders, and then she gave me that smile that still melts my heart every time.

Honestly, pruning this opportunity from our schedule was a no-brainer. When I'm at the end of my life looking back, that little bit of extra money won't mean much. I thought to myself, there's no price tag I could ever place on my relationship with Ashley and the time we have together. Giving up the money was a small but tangible way I could show her the place of priority she will always have in my heart.

So, what's that one thing a husband should do to make his wife happy? It goes back to what my dad said to me all those years ago. It's simply to prioritize your wife's needs ahead of your own agenda and schedule. It's to show her that you value your marriage more than your money. It's showing her that her joy brings you joy as well.

I fuel Ashley's happiness when she knows that I value her above any other career opportunity, relationship, pursuit, or agenda. When she knows that she doesn't have to compete with my career or hobbies for my time and attention, it gives her confidence and joy. When she knows I'm willing to prune my schedule for the good of our marriage, she feels protected and cherished. She deserves my best—not my leftovers. When I'm willing to give my best, she's much happier, and so am I.

Ashley

When we prune our schedules, we will have more time and energy to give our spouse. So often, there is tension in a marriage because of busyness. But don't nag or complain to your spouse about the pruning. Instead—*pray.* Together, ask God to give you the wisdom you need to know what needs to be pruned from your schedules (set aside for a different season) and what needs to remain.

God doesn't want us to prune our spouse, He wants us to pour into them. Instead of cutting away at them with our words, God wants us to pour into them words of life and encouragement. In the same way that water brings life and growth to a plant, our words need to bring life and nourishment to our spouses. As we are filled to overflowing by God and His love, we can't help but pour into our spouse. God is the Living Water, and He wants to funnel that water through us into our spouse. When we are rooted in Him, we can pour into our marriages the good fruits of joy, kindness, patience, and peace. So, as a couple, ask yourselves this—*What are you pruning and what are you pouring out?*

As a couple, you flourish by speaking words of encouragement and not criticism. Ephesians 4:32 reads,

"Be kind and compassionate to one another, forgiving each other, just as in Christ God forgave you."
(NIV)

Our words have power. We need to be our spouse's biggest encourager.

Our words have power to build up or to tear down, and the *tone* of our words will set the *tone* of our marriage. Dave and I counsel different couples who are struggling in their marriages, and many times one spouse will tell us, "Well, I don't really call them names or use swear words at them," and yet their spouse still feels hurt and disrespected. Sometimes, our *tone* sends a stronger message than our words. You may not use harsh words, but your tone of voice can be just as biting.

I've struggled with this over the years. Sometimes, I think I'm okay because I'm not using harsh words or name calling, but I can be so cold with my tone. I've learned to be aware of this because it can be easy to let that pass. I continually ask myself, *How is my tone? How am I communicating with Dave? Is my tone one of love and encouragement?* Truly, the tone of our words will set the tone of our marriage.

Not only is it important to think about what you are saying *to* your spouse, but it's also important to think about what you are saying *about* your spouse when they are not around. What do you say about your spouse when you get together with your girl friends or your guy friends? Is it a time when you are kind of trashing each other's spouses and talking about how they can't do anything right? Or how they are a nag or a ball and chain? These types of conversations create in our minds a negativity that we end up bringing home, and our spouse can sense the discord in the marriage.

We must focus on calling out the good in each other and speaking life over one another. Philippians 4:8 reads,

"And now, dear brothers and sisters, one final thing. Fix your thoughts on what is true, and honorable, and right, and pure, and lovely, and admirable. Think about things that are excellent and worthy of praise."
(NLT)

When we are looking for good things in our spouse, then we are going to see them a lot more. But if all we are looking for is the negative in our spouse, then that is precisely what we are going to find. Matthew 7:7 reads,

"Seek and you will find; knock and the door will be opened to you."
(NIV)

Whatever we are looking for we will find because we are focused on finding it.

If you train yourself to only see your spouse's flaws, then nothing they do will ever be good enough for you, and they will feel like a failure. Make sure you are looking for the right things. Negativity and criticism will never prompt our spouses to make the effort to improve. Instead of pouring encouragement into their souls, we are taking the pruning shears and hacking away at them. This doesn't create growth or change. Instead, it creates painful wounds.

What are we supposed to do when we are frustrated and feeling stuck because we want our spouse to change in a particular area? Nagging and complaining will never work. With good intentions, I hear wives say things like, "Oh, I just wish my husband would be the spiritual leader in our home." And yes, this is a *good* thing to desire; however, if we are nagging or complaining about it all the time then change won't happen. This will only make a husband feel like he can't win so he will think, *Why even try?* He may feel like his wife is wanting him to be like some of her favorite famous Bible teachers, leading two-hour Greek Bible studies, but this isn't how he is wired. Instead of trying to make him something he isn't, focus on what he does well and praise him for it.

Encouragement fuels the soul a lot more than criticism. If there is anything he is doing right in the area that you want him to grow—even if it seems insignificant to you, praise him for it. For example, if you want your husband to grow in the area of spiritual leadership, find something he is doing right in that area and praise it. If there is ever a Sunday when he is the one that says, "Let's all go to church today," then you go up to him, and say in your sultriest voice, "Babe, when you said, 'Let's go to church today' that was so attractive and sexy to me. I just love how you take the lead, and I'm so glad I married you."

He will feel like he is "the man," and he will be more inclined to want to go to church the following week. Find something to praise and encourage. This is biblical. God never called us to change someone through our criticism or nagging. Praised behavior is repeated behavior. Focus on the good, and the good will grow.

We're often guilty of showing more respect and thoughtfulness to strangers and coworkers throughout our day than we show to our spouse. There is no other human relationship more sacred than our marriage, so treasure your spouse and praise them.

I think sometimes spouses can think, *Well, I have this critical eye to see what others may not be able to see, and if no one tells them about their flaws, then they won't grow or change, so I better tell them.* Criticism often falls on deaf ears. So, let's think about how we can encourage our spouse instead. Look for the gold in your spouse and call that out in them through your praise. The more you praise your spouse, the faster they will grow and change. When we do this, our spouse flourishes and ultimately our marriage flourishes, which is the very heart of *Parah*—bearing fruit and thriving as a couple.

The only way for us to grow together in our marriages is to stay rooted in Christ through prayer, staying in the Word, and surrounding ourselves with other believers. When we choose to love and encourage our spouse the way Jesus loves them, our marriage will change. Don't treat your spouse the way they treat you; treat them the way God treats you.

Embrace the love of Jesus in your marriage and model the example of Jesus to your spouse. Jesus changed the world with love, and He wants us to continue this in our marriages. He wants to give you a new heart and new growth in your marriage. When you step from this life into eternity, love will be all that matters. Let God prune your life so that you can live with a heart of love. The results will amaze you!

10

NAKED FOREVER

Dave

There was a day when Ashley and I heard the word *Dad* in such a tone that it not only changed our lives forever, it changed our kids' lives forever too. *A lot of lives changed that day.* We were on a trip with our children, Ashley's parents, and her sister's family. Now, just as a note, we don't call these trips *vacations* because that would imply that *rest* was somehow involved, and we know *rest* isn't going to happen. So, we take trips.

On this particular trip, we rented a house in Hilton Head Island, South Carolina, and we shared it with Ashley's extended family. Ashley and I love these big family trips, but one of the challenges is that it's very hard to have any privacy—including any *special* mommy and daddy time, if you know what I mean. On a trip where you are already stressed and tired, if there isn't going to be any special marital bliss, then the trip is all the more difficult.

We thought it just wasn't going to happen. It was just going to be one of those kinds of trips. Lots of fun but no love-making. But suddenly, a window of opportunity emerged. The conditions were perfect: the baby was asleep, our older boys were playing video games, and everybody else was distracted. Ashley looked at me and said, "If it's ever going to happen, now is our chance." (She was never more beautiful to me than she was in that moment).

We were excited—maybe this trip wasn't going to be as

difficult as we thought! The only thing was that logistics were kind of a problem. We had the baby (who was a very light sleeper) sleeping in our room, so that was out. The only other option was our older boys' room. It was upstairs, and it had two twin beds. We thought, *We can make this work! It'll be fine.* So, we closed the door and we were sure to lock it. Now, as a quick side note, what I expect from a lock on a door is that once you lock it, it remains locked. It only has *one* job. That's it! That's all it has to do. But apparently, the homeowners of this establishment had a different definition of what a lock was supposed to do.

So, I locked the door. Then Ashley and I began to be very *loving* to one another, until all of a sudden, I felt this *waft* of air…that could only have been the *opening* of a door I was certain I had locked. Followed by this awkward silence… I didn't want to look, and Ashley just dove under the sheets! So, I was all alone when all of a sudden, I heard a terrified, shrill voice calling out, *"Dad? Dad is that you?!"*

I jumped up and wrapped myself in a sheet like a toga. My mind whirled in confusion as I just stood there and stammered, "What? What?!" He's looking at me, and I'm looking at him.

Neither of us knew what to say (There is no parenting book that prepares you for this moment). My twelve-year-old son surveyed the situation, along with his ten-year-old brother standing behind him, and with even more horror in his voice, he said, "Why did you have to pick *my* bed?!" (I don't think he slept the rest of the trip.)

At this point, he decided this was a moment that needed to be shared, so he yelled, "I'm telling Nana!" as he started to race down the stairs to alert the others that there was something upstairs they just needed to see.

In her most urgent voice, Ashley called out, "Catch him, Dave! He *cannot* tell Nana!" I started running, wrapped in the toga and doing the silent scream that all parents know, "Stop it! You cannot tell Nana!" Our lives were never the same from that day on. What our son simply wanted was to get something out of his room, but instead he got an image that will forever haunt his dreams.

I will say, there is one positive that came out of this experience. Now, when our son comes to our door and it's locked, he doesn't try to open it! In fact, Ashley and I hear him say with disgust, "Oh my gosh! Disgusting!" as he walks off. We all learned something, and now Ashley and I always triple check our door to make sure it's *really* locked!

Within reason, we think it's okay to gross out your kids sometimes. Ashley and I kiss and show affection in front of our kids, but for families where the kids never see their parents showing any affection, it's no wonder kids grow up having weird views about sex or about marriage in general. These kids are left thinking, *If my parents represent what marriage is, then I don't think I want it!*

The best gift you can give your kids is having the kind of marriage that makes them actually *want* to be married someday. Have the kind of marriage where they know Mom and Dad are going to be great when they leave the house, and they know you both enjoy spending time together. You want your kids to know that yes, you love spending time with them, but you also want to spend time alone with your spouse on a date night. And you show them that your marriage is a high priority when you spend time together and go on date nights. Also, letting your kids see you flirting with each other helps them to feel secure.

Ashley and I have had age-appropriate talks with our older boys about the topics of affection, marriage, and sex. So, when they see us embracing or sneaking in a little kiss, they may say something like, "Eww! Gross!" but we can see in their eyes and in their little smiles that they actually like seeing us being affectionate with each other. It brings them security because they know Mom and Dad really love each other.

Showing affection is part of the forever legacy that will

outlive you both. This legacy that creates a foundation for generations to come is the legacy of the love you have for each other and the love you have for God. What a powerful gift for future generations!

Ashley

When we are *legacy* minded it causes us to be fruitful, which influences others to want to be fruitful as well. It's a good thing for couples to want to leave a legacy together. When God was talking to Adam and Eve and told them to *Parah*, it's as if He was saying, "Eve, be so fruit-bearing in your life, so connected with Me, that you cause Adam to bear fruit and Adam, you do the same for Eve." When a couple does this, it influences others around them as well. As a couple, you influence others to bear fruit by serving in partnership with your spouse to make the world a better place.

God put the two of you together, not only for your pleasure, but for His pleasure too. God brought you together for a *greater purpose*. He brought you together so you could change the world in some way. You and your spouse are unique and special. There are no other people just like the two of you in this world, and together there are some great things God has for you and a distinct influence and mission that He has given you.

Many times we get caught up in the busyness or the mundaneness of life, and we start going through the motions. But when you understand that God has a calling He wants you to accomplish as a couple, your marriage rises to the next level. Remember, you are together for a greater purpose. Start having conversations where you ask, "What is the purpose God has for us? What is the legacy we will leave for the next generation?"

Of course, children are a part of this legacy, but Dave and I believe your legacy is even bigger than just you and your children. What are you planting as a couple that is impacting the lives of those around you and the world for God's glory? God's goal for you as a couple is for you to make the world a better place.

God has a global vision for your marriage. He wants you and your spouse to go out and create order out of chaos, create life where there is desolation, fill the world with love in places where there is hate and apathy, and bring peace where there is fear. Make this world a better place because you were here. Bring God's kingdom to earth. This is the mission we are called to. God doesn't just want to bless your marriage; He also wants to bless the world *through* your marriage.

God wants your life—your love story—to be something that outlives you. When you are in heaven, the ripple effect and the seeds you planted through your choices and actions will create a bountiful harvest that will change the world and impact generations. Whether we have children or not, we are all called to touch future generations through our words and our actions. As married couples, if we are not dreaming together or serving together then we are missing out on one of the most sacred and intimate parts of a marriage, something that will bind our hearts together and bring us both closer to God in the process.

There are countless examples of couples who have challenged us to think this way, but Dave and I want to share about one special couple who continues to inspire us, Dan and Lynn Smith. Dan is an ophthalmologist, and his wife Lynn works with him as they serve underprivileged children overseas. They truly are a remarkable example of bringing God's kingdom to earth as a couple. For several years now, Dan and Lynn have traveled to Casa Shalom Orphanage in Guatemala to minister to the children there. Dan and Lynn often go to the orphanage and give free eye exams and eye care to these children.

Many of these kids have never received eye care and if it wasn't for Dan and Lynn, they would never have the glasses they need. As you can imagine, these children come from dire situations and they desperately need treatment. Dan and Lynn go year after year, building relationships with the kids. Dave and I got to witness them at work firsthand and it was amazing.

We were able to tour the clinic where they help these kids. It was incredible to see Dan and Lynn serve these precious children with so much love and joy. They have even bigger plans for the future. After retirement, Dan and Lynn want to open an eye clinic in Guatemala, so they can help even more children.

It is awesome when you see a couple use the gifts and talents God has given them to show a child God's love and change the world for the better. The best marriages are couples who get this idea of serving and loving others for the glory of God's kingdom. This truly is how we leave a legacy that is bigger than ourselves.

Think big. Dream bigger. That's what God calls us to do. Just like Dan and Lynn, our marriages have a greater purpose. This is going to look different for every couple based on the talents, passions, and gifts God has given you. Keep dreaming together. Think about how you can serve others and change the world as a couple. Not only will this help your marriage, it will help the kingdom.

The happiest marriages are the ones where there is joy in partnering with God and the work He is doing to bring His kingdom to earth. Ask each other, "How can we change the world together?" You might start by serving together in children's ministry, leading a small group, or even just hosting a small group. Whatever it is for you, just start somewhere, and you will be amazed at what that does for your marriage and how it brings your hearts closer together to create a legacy that will last for eternity.

Dave

Creating a legacy together starts with commitment and consistency. Our commitment to our spouse is evident in the consistency with which we serve them. This is how legacies are created. Grand, one-time gestures can be nice, but it's what we do consistently to express love to our spouse that will ultimately shape our marriages and our legacies. Ashley and I met a couple who reminded us of the power of consistency and legacy in a beautiful way.

Harold and Louise are an extraordinary couple. Ashley and I had the privilege of meeting them at a marriage conference we hosted, and we were instantly drawn to them. There was a sparkle in their eyes and an adoration they obviously had for each other. They couldn't keep themselves from smiling every time their eyes met. Even though they were both in their seventies, they acted like two teenagers in love. They even wore matching shirts.

I spent as much time around them as I could that weekend because I wanted to learn the secret of their lifelong love. I wanted to know how their love had grown richer with time and how, even through painful setbacks in Louise's health, they both remained joyful, optimistic, and passionately devoted to each other. Louise now uses a wheelchair, but she looks like she could float on air when she looks at Harold.

When we asked this couple to tell us the secret to their lasting love, Louise shared a beautiful story that gave us a glimpse into their relationship: "Our first date was on March 17, so on April 17, Harold brought me a long-stem rose to celebrate our one-month anniversary. I was genuinely impressed by his thoughtfulness, but I didn't expect the roses to come very often. I was so surprised when he brought me another rose on May 17 to celebrate our second month together. I smiled and thought, *Wow! This fella is a keeper!*"

She looked at Harold with a smile and continued her story. "After we got married, I expected the roses to stop, but on the seventeenth of that first month of our marriage, another rose appeared."

She paused to squeeze Harold's hand, and tears began to form in her eyes as she smiled and said, "It has been fifty-four years since our first date, and every month on the seventeenth for 648 months in a row, Harold has brought me a rose."

As she finished, I was simultaneously inspired by their love story and feeling like a jerk for having never done anything for Ashley that could match that level of thoughtfulness. Harold definitely challenged me to raise the bar in my own marriage. I obviously couldn't build a time machine and go back to the beginning to start that type of tradition, but I can start today to bring more thoughtfulness and romance to the marriage. And you can too! We strengthen our legacies when we strengthen our marriage.

Harold and Louise would be quick to tell you it takes a lot more than roses to build a strong, lifelong legacy. The flowers weren't really even the point of their story; it was the thoughtfulness behind the flowers. As I spend time with couples who have successfully loved each other for decades, I'm convinced their secret is really no secret at all. It's a simple choice to put love into action by consistently serving, encouraging, supporting, and adoring each other. Make those simple but powerful acts of love a priority in your marriage, and you'll create your own legacy of love.

The commitment you make as a couple to serve and love others will define your legacy. Imagine how much richer and more vibrant your marriage could become if you asked God what *His* purpose is for your marriage. Love thrives where there is purpose. Embrace a deeper sense of responsibility for your marriage and cultivate a lasting legacy.

Maybe you are thinking, *Dave and Ashley, I haven't been living this way. I haven't cultivated a marriage that will leave a legacy.* If this is you, don't give up and don't let discouragement slow you down. It's never too late to start. Lamentations 3:23 reads,

"Great is his faithfulness; his mercies begin afresh each morning."
(NLT)

Don't give up! Start wherever you are. It just takes one choice—one prayer.

Several years ago, I received an encouraging message from God in a very unlikely way. This two-word message gave me hope, and I pray it does the same for you. I had just moved my family to a new city and was serving as a pastor in a new church. The transitions and pressures of life and ministry with a young family were beginning to feel overwhelming. I felt exhausted, misunderstood, frustrated, discouraged, and near the end of my rope. I wanted to quit. For the first time in my adult life, I wanted to do anything but ministry.

I was sharing all of this with Ashley one night, and finally in frustration I stood up from the couch and began to stomp around the living room like a toddler, saying, "God, it feels like you are being completely quiet right now! Where are you? I could really use a message from you. Just tell me what I'm supposed to do here!"

I looked down, and there was a sticker on my heel. It must have been left on the floor by one of my kids. As I peeled it off to look at it, I had to catch my breath. I was (and still am) convinced that sticker on my foot was a clear message from God. It simply read, "KEEP GOING!"

That marked a turning point in my attitude and my perspective. I wrote the date on that sticker and placed it on the front page of my Bible as a constant reminder. God gave me the strength to press through that difficult season, and very quickly, almost every area of life and ministry began to improve.

We've all had moments where we've felt like giving up and moments where we've wondered where God is in all of it. Maybe you're in one of those moments right now in your marriage, your work, or life in general. Ashley and I pray that you are reminded that God is with you, He is for you, He will carry you through the struggle, He will bring purpose from your pain, and He will reward your faithfulness with a lasting legacy. Just don't give up."

And let us run with endurance the race God has set before us. We do this by keeping our eyes on Jesus, the champion who initiates and perfects our faith
Hebrews 12:1–2 (NLT)

The legacy of love He is creating in and through your marriage is just getting started. Keep going until you reach the finish line!

Ashley

Are you dreaming together? What are the things you and your spouse are doing consistently to build toward that forever legacy? For Dave and me, we are constantly dreaming together and looking ahead at how we want to make an impact. We want our love to leave a lasting legacy.

We talk about what we want to do in the days ahead. For retirement, we don't want to just lie around, doing nothing for the last twenty years of our marriage, and we don't want to live in fear that we won't have anything in common when our kids grow up. Instead, we want to build our relationship every day.

You don't say, "I do," once. You say it every day. You wake up every day and say, "I do," again and again. And you do this by prioritizing time with each other. You go for walks together; you stay connected throughout the day by talking on the phone or texting. No matter what jobs Dave and I have had over the years, we talk or text all day long. Some people think we are weird because of this, but it helps us to stay connected and it keeps our vulnerability flowing. It keeps us on the path to being *naked* forever.

You will discover that the longer you go without doing life together, the more awkward you become with each other. Instead of connecting through real conversation, some couples just have "shop talk" or talk only about the business of life. That is why there is an epidemic of couples who raise their kids and then divorce. They weren't focused on each other—they were just co-parenting. Their marriage was business and not love. Now they have an empty nest *and* an empty marriage. This is a tragic reality that so many live in.

This is why Dave and I are so passionate about the *naked marriage*. Again, we didn't come up with this idea. God did. It's how He designed marriage. I think it's no mistake that Adam and Eve were naked and unashamed in the garden. They had no secrets between them. They didn't have anything hidden up their sleeves because they weren't even wearing sleeves.

They were naked in every way. Adam and Eve had no assumptions about each other. They had no preconceived notions. They were the first to exist and the first marriage. You don't see them trying to hide anything from each other or from God until sin enters the picture. Sin breeds secrets, but grace invites us back into that beautiful place of vulnerability.

Friends, ask yourselves, "What are the things we want to do together that will outlast us both?" When you are both in heaven, what will be the ripple effect from your love that will touch your children, your grandchildren, your church, and your community? As you dream and begin serving together, you will have a renewed commitment to the Lord and to each other.

Dave and I continuously encourage one another to think bigger. We want to know how God can use us in new ways. When we retire one day, we look forward to loving on our grandbabies, and we will also continue to ask God to show us how He wants us to make an impact in this world for His glory. He has a specific calling for all of us in *every* season. We just have to keep seeking Him and keep dreaming together.

I love seeing those couples who are technically retired, but they are serving at church together, or doing mission trips together, or maybe even starting a new business together that meets a need in the community. Whatever it is—have vision. Think bigger. Dream more and change your world through your *naked marriage*. When you do this, the love you have for God *and* the love you have for each other will outlast you both and make an eternal impact!

THE NAKED MARRIAGE

Ten-Week Discussion Guide for
Couples or Groups

To access the supporting
video sessions from
Dave & Ashley Willis visit

nakedmarriagebook.com/videos

DISCUSSION GUIDE: WEEK 1

Naked Is Good

This week's discussion questions are based on Chapter 1.

KEY VERSES:

Now the man and his wife were both naked, but they felt no shame.
—Genesis 2:25, NLT

A person standing alone can be attacked and defeated, but two can stand back-to-back and conquer. Three are even better, for a triple-braided cord is not easily broken.
—Ecclesiastes 4:12, NLT

KEY THOUGHT:

The strongest marriages are built on a foundation of love, vulnerability, and commitment.

DISCUSSION QUESTIONS:

1. As a child, what did you think marriage would be like?
2. Growing up, how did your parents represent sex and marriage? Were they openly affectionate like Dave's parents or more reserved like Ashley's parents?
3. How did your parents influence your views of love and vulnerability in marriage?
4. What does *The Naked Marriage* mean to you?
5. What would the "secret free guarantee" look like in your marriage?
6. How would your marriage benefit from more vulnerability?
7. In chapter 1, Ashley said, "We say, 'I do' every day to our spouse." What do you think she meant by this? What would saying, "I do" to your spouse every day look like in your marriage?

8. How would your marriage be different if it were the *naked marriage?* Would anything need to change?

APPLICATION QUESTION:

What is one area in my marriage where I can be more vulnerable (more naked) this week?

DISCUSSION GUIDE: WEEK 2

Naked Communication

This week's discussion questions are based on Chapter 2.

KEY VERSES:

We will speak the truth in love, growing in every way more and more like Christ.
–Ephesians 4:15, NLT

Understand this, my dear brothers and sisters: You must all be quick to listen, slow to speak, and slow to get angry.
–James 1:19, NLT

KEY THOUGHT:

In *a naked marriage,* broken relationships can be healed and strong marriages can grow stronger through honest communication.

DISCUSSION QUESTIONS:

1. Why is communication so important in marriage?
2. How is *communication* something we must work at regularly?
3. Ashley shared, "Daily heart-to-heart conversation is the cornerstone of true intimacy." Do you agree or disagree, and why?
4. What is one example of an assumption we might make in our marriages?
5. What is a marriage-building habit that you and your spouse can develop that would be worth imitating?
6. What is one decision or one new practice that you and your spouse can implement to alter the course of your marriage in a healthy way?
7. How can you and your spouse practically and consistently make talk-time together a priority?

8. How does the *tone* of your words shape the *tone* of your friendship and your marriage?

APPLICATION QUESTION:

How can you make communication a priority in your marriage this week?

DISCUSSION GUIDE: WEEK 3

Naked Fights

This week's discussion questions are based on Chapter 3.

KEY VERSES:

> *If it is possible, as far as it depends on you, live at peace with everyone.*
> —Romans 12:18, NIV

> *For we are not fighting against flesh-and-blood enemies, but against evil rulers and authorities of the unseen world, against mighty powers in this dark world, and against evil spirits in the heavenly places.*
> —Ephesians 6:12, NLT

KEY THOUGHT:

Hard times are when we need each other the most, and it's essential to know how to bring peace to any marriage conflict.

DISCUSSION QUESTIONS:

1. Have you ever felt like your marriage was stuck in a cycle of negativity? What was that like for you?
2. In the peace plan, the moment you feel frustration, you break the negative cycle by choosing forgiveness. How can you choose forgiveness during times of frustration?
3. Dave said, "If you're looking for your spouse's flaws, that's all you'll see; but if you're looking for the good, you'll start to see it." Do you agree? Why or why not?
4. Centuries ago St. Augustine said, "Holding a grudge is like drinking poison and then hoping the other person dies." What do you think he meant by this statement?
5. How might grudges and "keeping score" of faults poison your marriage?

6. Sometimes it's hard not to let your mind fixate on negativity. Why do you think this is?
7. How does choosing to forgive with grace look practically within marriage?
8. What is one new way you can pursue peace with your spouse during a time of conflict?

APPLICATION QUESTION:

What is one area of preference or perfectionism that you can let go of this week, in an effort to bring peace into your marriage?

DISCUSSION GUIDE: WEEK 4

Naked Sex

This week's discussion questions are based on Chapter 4.

KEY VERSES:

> *The husband should fulfill his marital duty to his wife, and likewise the wife to her husband. The wife does not have authority over her own body but yields it to her husband. In the same way, the husband does not have authority over his own body but yields it to his wife.*
> –I Corinthians 7:3–4, NIV

> *Kiss me and kiss me again! Your love is sweeter than wine.*
> –Song of Solomon 1:2, NLT

KEY THOUGHT:

Couples with the best sex lives have a man who continuously pursues, romances, and adores his wife and a wife who continuously affirms her husband and shows her respect and belief in him.

DISCUSSION QUESTIONS:

1. Why do you think sex can sometimes be such a hard thing to discuss openly and honestly?
2. What do you think is the kind of sex life that God wants us to have?
3. Did your parents represent sex as being positive or negative? Explain.
4. What does sex mean to you? And what would a healthy sex life look like in your marriage?
5. Dave and Ashley believe your marriage would benefit from more sex. Do you agree or disagree, and why?

6. What would happen if you and your spouse started having conversations with each other about sex? Would it be awkward? Or helpful? Explain.

7. How does having a sense of humor and not taking ourselves too seriously affect our sex lives? Is the result positive or negative? Explain.

8. If each spouse put the other spouse's needs ahead of his or her own needs, how would their sex life be impacted?

APPLICATION QUESTION:

How can you make sexual intimacy and fulfillment a priority in your marriage this week?

DISCUSSION GUIDE: WEEK 5
Naked Honesty
This week's discussion questions are based on Chapter 5.

KEY VERSE:

> *Do not lie to each other, since you have taken off your old self with its practices and have put on the new self, which is being renewed in knowledge in the image of its Creator.*
> —Colossians 3:9–10

KEY THOUGHTS:
Honesty has the power to set a positive course for your life and marriage, while also chasing away your fears in the process; true intimacy starts with naked honesty.

DISCUSSION QUESTIONS:
1. Why do you think most people have a problem with being completely honest?
2. How might secrecy be the enemy of intimacy?
3. What are some things that might hold you back from being completely honest with your spouse?
4. What does giving your spouse an all-access key to your heart, your mind, your hopes, your fears, and every other part of your life look like in your marriage practically?
5. How is honest communication important for a sexually fulfilling marriage?
6. Do you trust your spouse more or less when they have been honest with you in the past? Share about a time your spouse was honest and how that made you feel.
7. For you to feel safe enough to be completely honest with your spouse, what needs to happen?

8. Honesty is easier when you feel safe. What is one thing your spouse can do that would help you to feel safe enough to be transparent?

APPLICATION QUESTION:

This week have *naked honesty*. Is there something in your life that you need to confess to your spouse and to God?

DISCUSSION GUIDE: WEEK 6

Naked Scars

This week's discussion questions are based on Chapter 6.

KEY VERSES:

> *The Spirit of the Sovereign LORD is on me, because the LORD has anointed me to proclaim good news to the poor. He has sent me to bind up the brokenhearted, to proclaim freedom for the captives and release from darkness for the prisoners.*
> –Isaiah 61:1, NIV

> *He heals the brokenhearted and binds up their wounds. Great is our Lord, and abundant in power; his understanding is beyond measure.*
> –Psalm 147:3,5, ESV

KEY THOUGHT:

God wants to heal you so you can experience a loving marriage in its fullness.

DISCUSSION QUESTIONS:

1. When one or both spouses receive healing from past scars, how does it benefit the marriage?
2. How can we create an environment in the marriage where there is love and patience?
3. What does *emotional sunburn* mean to you? Are there areas in your life where you have had an *emotional sunburn*?
4. Can you identify a time in your life when your spouse unintentionally touched your *emotional sunburn*? How did you respond?
5. If you could bring healing to one part of your life or marriage, which part would you choose?

6. Starting today, how can you be intentional about healing from past scars? Share one practical step you can take.

7. What is one area in your marriage where you can help to promote healing through your love, encouragement, and prayers?

8. Jesus was the physical embodiment of love and healing, and He wants to heal our hearts—every scar, every heartbreak. Has there been a time in your life when you experience the healing power of Jesus either small or great? Share about this time.

APPLICATION QUESTION:

Scars heal when a husband and wife join in prayer and vulnerability. This week, what is one area you would like to experience the healing power of Jesus? Start praying for this area today!

DISCUSSION GUIDE: WEEK 7

Naked & Alone

This week's discussion questions are based on Chapter 7.

KEY VERSES:

> *Then the LORD God said, "It is not good for the man to be
> alone. I will make a helper who is just right for him."*
> –Genesis 2:18, NLT

> *For husbands, this means love your wives, just as Christ loved
> the church. He gave up his life for her.*
> –Ephesians 5:25, NIV

KEY THOUGHT:

Marriage mirrors the type of relationship God wants to have
with us: one of partnership, friendship, and unity.

DISCUSSION QUESTIONS:

1. Why do you think God said it isn't good for us to be alone?
2. What thoughts come into mind when you picture you and
    your spouse on the *loveseat* together? What does this look
    and feel like for you?
3. Think about a time you were in the *me-seat*; now think
    about a time you and your spouse were in the *loveseat*. How
    did you feel in the me-seat vs. the loveseat? What did you
    do differently when you chose to be in the loveseat?
4. If you were honest, do you feel like your marriage is more
    often in the *loveseat* or the *me-seat*? Explain.
5. How does serving one another in the loveseat represent
    how Jesus serves us?
6. What is one practical way you can commit to coming to
    the loveseat with your spouse no matter how you are
    feeling?

7. Think of a time when you were in the *loveseat* with your spouse. How did this influence your marriage?
8. Tell your spouse one specific area or thing they do that encourages you to want to be in the love seat together.

APPLICATION QUESTION:

What is the hardest challenge in your marriage? This week, commit to praying about this issue daily with your spouse.

DISCUSSION GUIDE: WEEK 8

Naked Forgiveness

This week's discussion questions are based on Chapter 8.

KEY VERSE:

Make allowance for each other's faults and forgive anyone who offends you. Remember, the Lord forgave you, so you must forgive others. Above all, clothe yourselves with love, which binds us all together in perfect harmony.
–Colossians 3:13–14, NLT

Love is patient, love is kind. It does not envy, it does not boast, it is not proud. It does not dishonor others, it is not self-seeking, it is not easily angered, it keeps no record of wrongs.
–I Corinthians 13:4–5, NIV

KEY THOUGHT:

Forgiveness is a choice, and both spouses must actively choose to forgive one another each and every day.

DISCUSSION QUESTIONS:

1. What does forgiveness mean to you and do you feel like it is important to marriage?
2. How is forgiveness like "sacred glue" that holds marriages together?
3. How does the practice of letting down our pride in the act of confession open the door for forgiveness?
4. What should you do in the marriage when a spouse refuses to apologize for broken trust or wrongdoing?
5. Do you view the act of apologizing as a form of strength or weakness? Explain.
6. How are trust and forgiveness different? How do you build trust after forgiving?

7. Ask your spouse, "What is one area I can grow in my level of trust with you?"
8. What is the best way for your spouse to demonstrate their sincerity when they apologize for a wrong doing?

APPLICATION QUESTION:
This week, what is one way you can build trust and vulnerability in your marriage?

DISCUSSION GUIDE: WEEK 9

Naked Purpose

This week's discussion questions are based on Chapter 9.

KEY VERSES:

Then God blessed them and said, "Be fruitful and multiply. Fill the earth and govern it."
−Genesis 1:28a, NLT

But the fruit of the Spirit is love, joy, peace, forbearance, kindness, goodness, faithfulness, gentleness and self-control. Against such things there is no law.
−Galatians 5:22–23, NIV

KEY THOUGHT:

Marriage is not simply about us. God has a purpose for our marriage to be fruitful.

DISCUSSION QUESTIONS:

1. What do you think a *fruitful* marriage looks like?
2. In Chapter 9, Dave writes, "Serving creates an antidote to the toxicity of complacency in marriage." Do you agree or disagree with this statement and why?
3. How does loving God increase our capacity to love our spouse?
4. What is one area in your life that you feel is the most fruitful and why?
5. What is one area in your life that you feel is the least fruitful and why?
6. What can you do differently to bring more fruitfulness into your life and marriage? How would this difference look practically each day?

7. Can you think of an example of a time you were influenced by someone else's commitment to *be fruitful*? Share about this time.

8. How would you like your marriage to influence those around you?

APPLICATION QUESTION:

This week, what is one area in your marriage that you and your spouse can prune in an effort to be more fruitful?

DISCUSSION GUIDE: WEEK 10

Naked Forever

This week's discussion questions are based on Chapter 10.

KEY VERSES:

> *Great is his faithfulness; his mercies begin afresh each morning.*
> –Lamentations 3:23, NLT

> *And let us run with endurance the race God has set before us. We do this by keeping our eyes on Jesus, the champion who initiates and perfects our faith.*
> –Hebrews 12:1–2, NLT

KEY THOUGHT:

The happiest marriages are the ones where there is joy in partnering with God and the work He is doing to bring His kingdom to earth.

DISCUSSION QUESTIONS:

1. Are you dreaming together? If yes, what are you dreaming about?
2. What was the legacy that your parents or grandparents passed to you?
3. Which legacies from your family do you want to continue and why? Which legacies from your family do you *not* want to continue and why?
4. What is the legacy you and your spouse want to leave for the next generation?
5. What are the things you and your spouse are doing consistently to build towards that forever legacy?
6. Think of a time when you and your spouse served others together. What was this like for you both? Share about this experience.

7. What are some natural gifts and talents that you and your spouse have that can serve your church family and your community?

8. What do you think is the purpose God has for your marriage?

APPLICATION QUESTION:

What are the things you and your spouse want to do together that will outlast you both? (Think big!)

ACKNOWLEDGMENTS

There are so many people who have impacted our own story and also have helped give life to this book. Before we list out some important friends, colleagues and mentors who have shaped *The Naked Marriage*, we want to thank YOU for taking the time to read our story. By reading, applying and sharing the message of this book, you've partnered with us in this work of building stronger marriages. Thank you!

Though her name is not on the cover, the influence of our writing partner Sarah Wronko can be seen on every page. Thank you, Sarah, for helping bring life to our story. You did a fantastic job!

Our deepest gratitude and appreciation goes to Jimmy and Karen Evans and Brent and Stephanie Evans. We are truly honored to call you friends and we're equally honored that you've adopted us into the *MarriageToday* family! Thank you for your ongoing guidance, encouragement and support.

Thanks to the entire staff and Marriage Coaches team at *MarriageToday* and *XO*. We love you guys and are so thankful to get to do life and ministry alongside you. Specifically for the hard work related to this book, we'd like to thank fellow team members Scott and Leah Silverii, Joni Smith, Ashley Ziegler, Derek Nelson, Chelsea Green and Hailey Rojas. On the tech side, we'd also like to thank Brittany Wilcox, Jordan Kennedy, Marcus Bowen, Jonathan Armbruster and Chris Stetson for your stellar work producing, *The Naked Marriage Podcast* and this book's accompanying video series.

We are eternally grateful for the love and support of our family. We want to thank our parents, Brad and Karen Willis and Bill and Mary McCray for your lifelong love and support. We also want to thank our siblings and our extended family for all you do for us. Special thanks to our precious sons Cooper, Connor, Chandler and Chatham. We love you boys and all we do we do for you. The greatest honor in our lives is the privilege of being your parents. We also want to thank the world's best babysitter, Cara Griffith, who has become an adopted part of our family and she loves our kids like her own when we're traveling for ministry events.

We'd also like to show our appreciation to Dr. Marty Baker and the entire church family at Stevens Creek Church in Augusta, GA. Although we've moved away, you'll always be our church home away from home and your impact in our lives and our ministry is immeasurable. Thank you for your continued prayers, encouragement, text messages, Facebook shout-outs and a million other little things that mean more than you'll ever know. We love you guys.

Our heartfelt gratitude also extends to our friends near and far who have helped shape the content of this book through your stories, your encouragement and your prayers. For those social media friends who we've never met in person but who have encouraged us, prayed for us and shared our content with others, please know that your impact in this ministry and in our lives is profound. Thank you for your partnership in this work of building stronger marriages and pointing more people to God's love, grace and peace.

Finally and most importantly, we want to thank Jesus Christ, our Lord and Savior. He is the giver of all good things. It's all for His glory.

ABOUT DAVE AND ASHLEY

Dave and Ashley Willis have become two of America's most trusted voices on issues related to marriage, faith and family. They are part of the team at *MarriageToday* which is the nation's largest marriage ministry. Dave and Ashley's videos, articles, books, podcasts and live events reach millions of couples worldwide. They live with their four young sons near Dallas, TX. For additional resources, please visit DaveAndAshleyWillis.com.